Audrey Zenner, in her impressive and incredibly valuable workbook, "Precise American Writing," has filled an important gap in the education of international students in terms of their academic writing. Her work not only is a valuable and practical educational resource, but it will also encourage American universities and colleges to pay greater attention to the writing styles of this diverse group of students.

W. Clarke Douglas, Ph.D.
Associate Vice Chancellor for Student Affairs
Associate Adjunct Professor of History
University of Illinois at Chicago
Chicago, Illinois, U.S.A.

Audrey Zenner's method of instruction is both incisive and gentle. In a tone that is encouraging and unfailingly positive, this book cuts straight to the information that non-native English academic writers must need to know, as well as those issues that most commonly confuse these writers.

With that knack many strong educators hold, she is able to strongly relate to her international students while offering the point-of-view of the American academic community that will eventually serve as her students' critical audience.

Patrick Koerner, M.A. in English
Former Assistant Director
Academic Center for Excellence
University of Illinois at Chicago
Chicago, Illinois, U.S.A.

I have found "Precise American Writing" to be a smooth prose that engages writing instructors, as well as, their students. This book provides students with a simple and refined framework for thinking as college writers. Audrey Zenner has indeed filled in a niche at an affordable price. My writing students have found this book to be a simple and painless way to improve their academic writing skills. If I recommend one book on academic writing to all my students- this is it!

Bahar Baniasad, M.A.
Instructor, English as a Second Language
Academic Center for Excellence
University of Illinois at Chicago
Chicago, Illinois, U.S.A.

PRECISE AMERICAN WRITING

A Guide for International Students and Professionals

Audrey Zenner, M.A.

Marsten Publishing Group, LLC

Naperville, Illinois, USA

Marsten Publishing Company books may be purchased for educational, business, or personal use. For information on other books, please write: Literary Department, Marsten Publishing Group, LLC, 1750 W. Ogden Ave., #5308, Naperville, IL 60567, or visit www.marstenpublishing.com.

Printed on acid-free paper.

Library of Congress Control Number: 2012955770

ISBN: 978-0-9820678-3-3

THIS BOOK IS DEDICATED

to my daughter, Angel Britt

She guides me,

She loves me,

She inspires me,

so that I can better understand our universe.

TABLE OF CONTENTS

INTRODUCTION BY THE AUTHOR

This text offers basic suggestions and examples to guide one towards successful academic writing. The impetus for creating this book began as various writing handouts for international students and visiting scholars. They urged me to publish this book since it was so useful to them. As a matter of fact, these students also critiqued the material as they worked through the pages during our classes. Initially, each section presents an explanation for the topic introduced; followed by examples; practical exercises using the target writing lesson; and concluding with a final written sample. Therefore, this text may also be utilized as a workbook. The section topics were selected by consensus of importance by my students. Notably, students from every corner of the world have contributed to this book. Plus, diverse fields of study have been taken into consideration; such as, nursing, additional health fields, engineering, computer science, accounting, business, communications, economics, and political science, just to name more than a few.

SECTION 1

Academic

Writing

Overview

American writing styles in academia differ significantly from other countries. As international students, you bring unique sociolinguistic backgrounds to the United States which may pose setbacks in English accuracy; yet, conscientious effort can resolve this. While many American university instructors may not be familiar with individual cultural mindsets, as our international students increase in number, we are ever striving to be sensitive and responsive to diverse needs.

Our writing stresses clear communication in a succinct manner. We do not infer meaning, as other cultures may do so out of respect. Additionally, vague terminology has no place in American academic writing. We strive for explicit words; whereby, allowing your reader to interpret factual meaning through your writing. Complex sentence structures and overt formal language are not necessary in attempting to impress your professors. Remember, less is more! Furthermore, our rich English vocabulary allows for linguistic manipulation to achieve your goals. In order to guide the reader, we aim for good flow throughout the paper. After introducing the main idea at the beginning of the paper, we follow an outline that maintains our focus while demonstrating the important points. Within the paragraphs, transitional words are utilized to guide the reader toward new ideas, comparisons, contrasts, time sequences, restatements, and conclusions. As a result, smooth flow of your ideas will contribute to good coherence throughout your text, allowing for logical presentation.

Typically, the main topic (main idea) is introduced in the first paragraph of your text. The following paragraphs lend support to this topic, concluding with a short summarization at your closing. The subsequent outline is a very simplistic view, outlining this format; of course, this design can be expanded upon to include other sections and sub-sections.

SAMPLE OUTLINE

paragraph #1   *introduction, stating main idea within thesis statement*

paragraph #2   *point 1, lending support*

paragraph #3   *point 2, lending support*

paragraph #4   *point 3, lending support*

paragraph #5   *conclusion*

Assuredly, language learning is a lifetime session. Attaining skills in American academic writing will certainly sustain you throughout a successful career. I hope this text will ease your pursuit in writing.

Formal Grammar and Style

		Informal	Formal
1.	Avoid contractions.	Can't Won't	Cannot Will Not
2.	Use formal negatives	not + verb + any not + verb + much not + verb + many	verb + no (We have no homework.) verb + little (We have little time.) verb + few (We have few choices.)
3.	Place adverbs within the verb. (Not at the beginning or end.)	It was driven slowly. Then it can be utilized.	It was <u>slowly</u> driven. It can <u>then</u> be utilized.
4.	Limit the use of direct questions.	What should be done to ameliorate the problem?	Ways to ameliorate this problem must be considered. *OR* A solution to this problem must be devised.
5.	Limit the use of commands.	Now consider this case.	This case must be fully considered.
6.	Do not use "run on" expressions.	and so forth, etc., and so on	Everything written in formal grammar and style must be fully explained.
7.	Do not focus on the reader.	you, your, you guys, you all, y'all, yous guys you'uns	If necessary, you may use the word, "one" in place of you. For example: One may find success in scholarly research.
8.	Try not to focus on the writer.	I, me, my, mine, we, us, our, ours	For example: I focused on my research during the summer.-NO During the summer, focused research ruled.-YES-
9.	Do not use idioms.	To lend a hand. In hot water.	To help. In trouble.
10	Never use slang.	Don't get bent out of shape. Don't blow your cool.	Do not get so upset. Do not become so angry.

Exercise 1A - Formal Versus Informal Wording

In the following pairs, circle the item considered as accurate formal usage in an academic paper.

1.	kids	children
2.	will not	won't
3.	father	pop
4.	&	and
5.	How come?	Why?
6.	application	app
7.	couldn't	could not
8.	humongous	large
9.	quote	quotation
10.	lift	ride
11.	It was eaten quickly.	It was quickly eaten.
12.	Consider the following data.	The following data may be considered.
13.	He ordered fish, chips, salad, etc.	He ordered fish, chips, and salad.
14.	What can we do to solve the problem?	There are many ways to solve the problem.

Word Choice - Formal Grammar and Style

By simply right-clicking on most words in Word, make note of the synonyms listed on the drop down menus. By using this, you may vastly improve your English vocabulary.

1.   The university has made *good* progress in assessing teacher needs.

     Informal English.

     (excellent, superior, high rate of, first-rate)

2.   We *got* results that differed from *what we wanted*. This is informal,

     conversational English.

     (obtained, attained, acquired, achieved)   (our goals, objectives, targets)

3.   The results from *a lot of* developments have been *pretty good*. Informal,

     conversational English.

     (many, numerous, several, various)   (optimal, favorable, positive,

     constructive, encouraging)

4.   Job loss is one of the *things that will happen* if this program is *set up*.
     Informal, conversational English.

     (will transpire, will become apparent/obvious)   (established, created,

     launched)

5.   The reaction of the people was *kind of* positive. (generally, typically)
     Informal, conversational English.

6.   The weather forecast is *looking good*. (positive, optimistic)   Idiom.

7.   The program's future is *up in the air*. (undecided, unsure)   Idiom.

8.   Many different facets of the auto industry *are planning to*   Too wordy.

get together on the research needed for electric automobiles.

(plan on meeting, will meet)

9.   The rules are not *written in stone*.   Idiom.

(definite, crystal clear)

10.   He *changed a bunch of stuff* on his computer.   Informal,
conversational English.

(modified/altered/adjusted many things)

Exercise 1B – Word Choice

Substitute the word in parentheses with more suitable academic English words.

1. Begin each day with a nourishing breakfast to keep you going (strong) _____ all day.

2. Low calorie diets are a (good) _____ approach to losing weight.

3. Athletes usually (eat) _____ high protein foods to sustain their energy levels.

4. Remember to always drink plenty of water to keep your body (well) _____ hydrated.

5. (Regular) _____ exercising helps to maintain an efficient metabolism.

6. Concentrate on walking each day to keep your weight down and your life (long) _____.

7. Pedometers are small gadgets used to (measure) _____how many steps you walk in a given time period.

8. Fuel your metabolic engine by eating and drinking something every 3 -4 hours (throughout) _____ the waking hours.

9. Cross-training (allows) _____ you to focus on different body areas, being ever mindful of not concentrating on the same area too much.

10. It's common (knowledge) _____ that a good workout will reward you with a better night's sleep.

DO USE

3rd person

formal academic language

transitions

action verbs

check grammar

proofread aloud

DON'T USE

contractions (won't, don't, etc.)

commands (Write this, remember that)

fragments (incomplete sentences)

run-ons (2 or more sentences lacking punctuation and/or connecting words)

informal language or slang (colloquial speech)

idioms

wordiness (no ornate language, unnecessary words to increase the number of words, redundancy, & overuse of difficult terminology)

vague language (strive for accurate meaning)

passive voice (i.e., The briefcase *was carried by* the professor.)

bullets & lists

plagiarism

personal writing (do not focus on yourself, but the topic)

slang

Formal Academic Language

As you proceed in writing, you will want to adapt a clear, concise manner of expressing your ideas within a formal context of words. In order to inhibit your reader from having to infer meaning, you will proceed to build a rich lexicon within your field of study for both the general public and experts. Aim to avoid informal wording and slang. Your subject area textbooks usually maintain a detailed glossary of specific vocabulary. Through time, these words will function as tools of your trade in writing abstracts, essays, research papers, and articles. It's always best to learn new vocabulary within context, so take full advantage of this resource. Above and beyond studying your assigned textbooks, become familiar with journal articles being published in your area of expertise. While reading, make mental notes of the author's style of writing, format, vocabulary, and general tone (manner and characteristics of the text). The more you read in English, the better you will adapt to writing in this target language. Practice makes perfect!

Surely, with the use of strong words, you are enabling your reader to gain a more realistic visualization of your ideas through the words you have chosen. Gaining the reader's attention and holding it is not an easy task, but well worth the effort. Try not to use every day nouns that we may use in conversation. Endeavor to replace those words with discerning nouns that transmit more meaning to your text. Descriptive adjectives can assist you in enhancing your nouns, while adverbs may fittingly add dimension to your verbs. As an alternative in choosing passive verbs, draw on strong action verbs to communicate a vivid picture within the text. Below, is a sampling of such strong verbs:

Strong Verbs

abandon   accelerate   access   accompany   accumulate   achieve

adhere   adjust   administer   advocate   affiliate   agitate   aid

align   allege   allude   alter   analyze   approach   assess

assume   author   captivate   champion   comply   conclude

consolidate   construct   consult   critique   define   denote

derive   devise   direct   enhance   equate   establish   evaluate

exceed   face   forge   formulate   generate   guarantee

identify   illustrate   impact   imply   indicate   initiate

interpret   involve   maximize   optimize   pioneer

presume   structure   sum   vary

Sample sentences:

1. The professor **wrote** many vital articles for a leading journal in chemical engineering.

   *The professor **authored** many vital articles for a leading journal in chemical engineering.*

2. We **began** our research with various experiments in the laboratory.

   *We **established** our research with various experiments in the laboratory.*

3. The chemistry students **studied** the current research assigned by their professor.

   *The chemistry students **analyzed** the current research assigned by their professor.*

4. *When will we **start** our class project?*

   *When will we **initiate** our class project?*

5. *You may **form** your own opinions after all evidence is presented.*

   *You may **structure** your own opinions after all evidence is presented.*

6. *The research team **changed** the course's direction quite abruptly.*

   *The research team **altered** the course's direction quite abruptly.*

7. *The Biochemistry Department was ordered to **combine** all graduate classes within 500 level course sections.*

   *The Biochemistry Department was ordered to **consolidate** all graduate classes within 500 level course sections.*

8. *The students were **angry** about their poor grades on the exam.*

   *The students were **agitated** about their poor grades on the exam.*

Strong Action Verbs

As an alternative to employing weak or passive verbs in your writing, liven it up with strong action verbs, while increasing your vocabulary.

advocate	encourage, promote
author	write
captivate	hold your interest
champion	defend, support
consolidate	combine, join
critique	review, analyze
depart, proceed	go
diversify	expand
divert	switch, avert
enhance	increase, develop
exceed	go over, go beyond
pioneer	lead the way
forge	build
formulate	invent, originate
generate	make, produce
inspire, persuade	have influence
initiate	begin, start
integrate	put together, mix
intensify	increase, strengthen
exist, remain, occur, transpire	to be (is)
mastermind	plan, organize
maximize	make the most of
orchestrate	arrange, organize
spearhead	lead
structure	put together, make up
proliferate	reproduce, grow
recapture	bring back
rejuvenate	make younger
employ, operate	use
print	publish

Choosing the Correct Verb

Quite often, when searching the dictionary for an appropriate verb, several synonyms are given; yet, they are not interchangeable since their meanings may vary considerably. How do you know which verb to choose? Of course, if you have adequate experience with some verbs, those are not problems. First of all, use an American English to English dictionary and/or thesaurus; whereby, restricting yourself to standard American English. Second of all, look at what is going on in the given sentence. The verb must be appropriate for the specific meaning in that sentence. For instance, the verb *cook* has various synonyms: *prepare, boil, stew, simmer, parboil, brew, poach, bake, roast, toast, fry, sauté, braise, brown, broil, grill, barbecue, steam, and baste.* All of these words do not mean the same and are very different.

Dad *poached* the hamburgers on the barbecue last night.

No way! (*Poach* means to lightly boil in water.)

Dad *grilled* the hamburgers on the barbecue last night.

Yes!

Mom *braised* the bread for breakfast this morning.

No way! (*Braise* means to cook food, meat or vegetables, by browning briefly in hot oil, adding a little liquid, and cooking at a low temperature in a covered pot.)

Mom *toasted* the bread for breakfast this morning.

Yes!

Exercise 1C – Replace the incorrect verb by circling the better choice.

1. The rice was *barbecuing* in its cooker for 45 minutes.

    broiling, steaming

2. After rolling out the dough, we put the bread in the oven to *fry*.

    bake, brew

3. Class, *snoop* attentively to your wise teacher until lunch time.

    eavesdrop, listen

4. *Stare at* the actors on stage when they take a bow.

    watch, keep a lookout for

5. Lucy *spooned out* the soup into her mouth.

    served, spooned

6. The toddler *sketched* a picture of a clown.

    drew, illustrated

7. Most of the kindergarten class was able to *engrave* their names.

    inscribe, write

8. All morning, the family *heaved* weeds from the garden.

    pulled, lugged

9. My head of hair needs to be *raked through*.

    scrutinized, combed

10. *Sweep* your teeth after every meal.

    brush, scrape

EXERCISE 1D– Verb Match

Match the weaker verb with the stronger verb by entering the matching weak verb number in the space provided:

COMMON WEAK VERBS

STRONG VERBS

1. be different	establish _____
2. see, discover	derive _____
3. go ahead	generate _____
4. get rid of	illustrate _____
5. join	accumulate _____
6. collect	vary _____
7. show	proceed _____
8. make	abandon _____
9. get	identify _____
10. start	consolidate _____

EXERCISE 1E – Noun Match

Match the weaker noun with the stronger noun by entering the matching weak noun number in the space provided:

WEAK NOUNS	STRONG NOUNS	
1. review	verdict	_____
2. area	contemplation	_____
3. decision	evaluation	_____
4. answer	declaration	_____
5. control	response	_____
6. shame	domain	_____
7. activity	moderation	_____
8. sign	precursor	_____
9. thought	animation	_____
10. statement	indignity	_____

EXERCISE 1F – Noun Match

Using the word bank, match the weaker noun with the stronger noun by writing in the blank space.

WORD BANK
STRONG NOUNS

disease   procedure   suggestion   dilemma   metropolis

article   lure   magnitude   response   nation

COMMON WEAK NOUNS   **STRONG NOUNS**

city   _____

country   _____

illness   _____

importance   _____

method   _____

idea   _____

item   _____

problem   _____

answer   _____

attraction   _____

EXERCISE 1G – Strong Nouns

WORD BANK

Strong Nouns

recollection   application   occurrence   exemplifications

distinction   blizzard   prominence   proposals

compliance   divergences   revelation

Using the word bank, cross out the weak noun and write the stronger noun in its place.

On my way to class today, my *(memory)* _____ of cool winter days in southern China was altered by the *(experience)* _____ of snowflakes transforming the blue sky to white. What a remarkable *(discovery)* _____! I was witnessing my very first *(snowstorm)* _____. In the past, I had never experienced such *(examples)* _____ of weather. My whole attitude toward cold wintertime conditions changed before my eyes; my *(willingness)* _____ increased to comprehend harsh seasonal realities. This topic deserves *(merit)* _____ given that a large portion of human beings must adapt to extreme *(differences)* _____ in weather throughout the year. The *(importance)* _____ of following through with winter *(plans)* _____ to insure clearing the snow, heating buildings, and maintaining warm attire, is vital. Fortunately, our national weather sources keep us well informed of impending weather conditions.

Writing for an Academic Audience

For whom are you writing? Who is going to read your paper and why? You must identify your audience to be a successful writer. Consider the following two questions.

> *Is your audience less knowledgeable about the subject matter you are presenting?*

> *Is your audience more knowledgeable about the subject matter you are presenting?*

The audience with less knowledge than you requires that your writing purpose be one of instruction. A case in point may be how a teacher writes for students, instructional writing.

The audience with more knowledge than you requires that your writing purpose be one of demonstrating your intellect, knowledge, and proficiency on the subject matter. A student writing an academic paper for coursework would be suitable for such writing.

Take a look at the two sample sentences below and consider who the audience might be; consequently, distinguishing the purpose for each piece of writing.

1. *Linguistics is a broad field involving the study of language.*

2. *Linguistics is the science of language, comprised of morphology, phonetics, phonology, syntax, semantics, pragmatics, and historical linguistics.*

Word choice and tone need to fit the expectations of your audience. What is the most important idea you are trying to put into words? Your aim should be for clear communication.

1.   *(Less knowledgeable audience)*
2.   *(More knowledgeable audience)*

Name
Date
Course

Paragraph Outline Form

Title: _____

Topic sentence:_____
                    (Include main idea.)

_____.

Support1:_____

_____.

Support 2: _____

_____.

Support 3: _____

_____.

**Concluding
sentence**:_____

_____.

(Be sure to mention your main idea once again in your concluding sentence.)

21

Editing Table

As can be seen in the following Editing Table, common symbols are used to designate corrections to be made. More than likely, when submitting a first draft paper for consideration, you will receive it back marked with some of these editing symbols. These symbols will point to specific words, punctuation, and articles which need to be corrected by you. As a result, you will correct all of the errors pointed out and then resubmit your second draft paper.

For example: *School is where student could expand horizons and grow to be valuable asset to society.*

Corrected version: School is where **a** student **can** expand **his/her** horizons and grow to be **a** valuable asset to society.

Explanation:

- The first error is a missing article **a** and would be marked with *art*.

- The second error is the wrong verb tense (past – could) which was corrected to the present verb tense **can** and would be marked with *vt*.

- The third error is a case of missing pronouns which show possession **his/her** and would be marked with *pro*.

- The fourth error is a missing article **a** and would be marked with *art*.

EDITING SYMBOLS

wf	word form
count	non-count noun
sing	singular noun problem
pl	plural noun problem
wo	word order – incorrect/awkward
ww	wrong word
pro	pronoun agreement
?	unclear
s/v	subject/verb agreement
vt	verb tense
vf	verb format
verb?	verb missing
modal	modal use
punct	punctuation (period, comma, semicolon, etc.)
cap	capitalization
prep	preposition
conj	conjunction
R O	run-on sentences–too long of a sentence; reduce or
frag	Sentence fragment – partial sentence
art	article
para	paragraph format problem
sp	Spelling

YOUR NOTES

SECTION 2

Bio-Statement

Writing Titles Properly

- Always capitalize the important words in the title.

  Precise American Writing

- books (full-length) (preferred) OR <u>underline</u>

  italics

  Title of the Book, <u>Title of the Book</u>

- periodical, newspapers (preferred) OR <u>underline</u>

  italics

  The Chicago Tribune, <u>The Chicago Tribune</u>

- long reports/documents (preferred) OR <u>underline</u>

  italics

  Public Speaking Documents, <u>Public Speaking Documents</u>

- shorter documents or not at all

  quotation marks

  "Bi-Weekly Report," Bi-Weekly Report

- articles of newspapers & periodicals

  quotation marks
  "Illinois' Report Card," "Popular Mechanics"

- short story, play, poem, musical, movie, TV, or radio program, art, short literature

quotation marks
"The Red House on the Hill,"
"After the Rain,"
"Titanic,"
"Friends"

*Please check the writing style (for example: APA, MLA, Chicago, etc.) that your field of study uses since they have their own rules on writing titles.

BIOGRAPHICAL STATEMENTS

Our writing coursework commences with a simple paragraph that demonstrates how American English paragraphs are organized. At times, you may be asked to write a brief professional description of yourself when submitting a paper for publication. Conferences or journals quite often request short biographical statements from the people presenting or publishing. The format of this writing goes from general to specific; whereby, proceeding with identification by name, title and place of work. Consequently, one supplies highlights of his/her working career. Guide your reader along with supportive information which becomes more specific and always be attentive to chronological order. Remember to be concise and clear in communicating your ideas; at the same time, avoid wordiness. An outline of our paragraph consists of

1) the topic sentence

2) three sentences supporting the topic

3) the concluding sentence

The first sentence in this *biostatement* is a topic sentence which tells the main idea of what you are writing. Subsequently, the next three sentences provide support for your topic. Finally, your fifth and last sentence briefly summarizes or proposes an idea for the future.

Sample biostatement in outline form:

TOPIC SENTENCE

Dr. Susan Study has taught and researched linguistics and second language acquisition for the past 30 years.

SUPPORT SENTENCE

She graduated from the University of Illinois at Chicago (UIC) with a BA/English, MA/Linguistics, and PhD/Linguistics.

SUPPORT SENTENCE

Since 2000, Dr. Study has been a member of the UIC faculty and instructed various courses in her area of expertise.

SUPPORT SENTENCE

Additionally, her research in second language acquisition is highly regarded and published throughout a range of journals.

CONCLUDING SENTENCE

Dr. Susan Study's future research plans consist of studying and teaching abroad.

Sample biostatement in paragraph form:

Dr. Susan Study has taught and researched linguistics and second language acquisition for the past 30 years. She graduated from the University of Illinois at Chicago (UIC) with a BA/ English, MA/ Linguistics, and PhD/Linguistics. Since 2000, Dr. Study has been a member of the UIC faculty and instructed various courses in her area of expertise. Additionally, her research in second language acquisition is highly regarded and published throughout a range of journals. Dr. Susan Study's future research plans consist of studying and teaching abroad.

Helpful Suggestions

- Do not add information that implies a personal relationship in professional business, for example, "I worked in my father's business."

- Be careful with your usage of articles (a, an, the).

- Write in the 3rd person singular (your name and/or he/she).

- Do not write in the 1st person – I.

- For now, position your transitional words at the beginning of the sentence followed with a comma.

- Do not use acronyms, spell everything out. No contractions.

- Be careful with usage of prepositions.

- Use spell-check, plus take note of the red, green, and blue underlining in Word.

- Only highlight aspects of your professional/academic career, not activities.

Bio-statement Review Exercise

Go over this checklist to help in your review.

1. Chronology (events in order of occurrence) must be ascending order (upward) or descending order (downward). Does the chronology make sense or does the bio-statement jump all over?

2. How about the verb tenses?

    ➤ have worked *(worked for some time before now)*

    ➤ have been working (worked for a specific time in progress in the past)

    ➤ had worked *(worked before another time in the past)*

    ➤ worked *(simple past)*

    Make sure the tense matches the time being written about.

3. Are there any gaps? Is "UIC" OK? Would the reader understand "UIC"?

    Is there anything missing that should be included?

4. Is there any information that should be eliminated?

5. Be concise. Be clear. Is there any place that you can reduce the amount of words and express the same idea? Is there any place that the reader might be confused?

    e.g.   She has received her Master's Degree in Economics from UIC four years ago.

    Is the verb tense correct? When is *four years ago*? When will the bio-statement be published?

Make it a definite time so you can repeat the bio-statement in the future.

She received her Master's Degree in Economics from the University of Illinois (UIC) in 2008.

e.g. He was a second lieutenant in the Marines while completing his military service.

Too wordy. *While completing his military service* is not needed. The first clause should be combined with the preceding or following sentence.

After serving in the Marines as a second lieutenant, Mr. Smith ....

SAMPLES OF BIOSTATEMENTS

(with possible errors)

1.

Stella Student is a graduate student in the master's program, Instructional Leadership at the University of Illinois at Chicago. She taught the bilingual course of both Chinese and English in the Irvine Chinese School in 2007. She holds a Bachelor's Degree in Education from National Chengchi University, (NCU), 2006. As a student at NCU, she received the President Award in her junior year. She worked in the Humanistic Education Foundation and was also a leader in an underserved children's program, Love Education Camp. (81 words)

2.

Stephanie Student is a PhD student in Electrical and Computer Engineering at the University of Illinois at Chicago. Her current research topic is video classification. She is mainly interested in video processing, video retrieval and image analysis. She received her MS and BS in Automation from Shanghai Jiao Tong University, China. (50 words)

3.

Stacy Student is a PhD candidate with the Urban Planning and Policy Program at the University of Illinois at Chicago. She received a Master of Science in Urban and Regional Planning from Florida State University. Her current research interest focuses on the use of advanced technology to help increase transit ridership. (47 words)

4.

Stuart Student received the B.S. Degree in Electrical Engineering from the University of Science and Technology of China, Hefei, China, in 2005. Subsequently, he was admitted into the PhD program in the Department of Electrical and Computer Engineering, the University of Illinois at Chicago, Illinois, (UIC). There, while studying as a PhD candidate, he worked as a research assistant in the multimedia communications lab, UIC. He has authored eight technical papers in various journals and served regularly as a reviewer for different journals and conferences, such as IEEE Transactions on Image Processing and IEEE Transactions on Circuits and Systems for Video Technology. (99 words)

5.

Sylvia Student is a professor of Nursing College, Gyeongsang National University (GNU), South Korea. Also, she is a general nurse practitioner in South Korea, and a registered nurse in New York, USA. Her specialty is gerontology nursing. Her research focuses mainly on health promotion strategy including development and evaluation of exercise programs for older adults. Also, she has been a member of the gerontology health research center at GNU. She earned a BS, MS, and PhD in nursing from Seoul National University, South Korea. She is a visiting scholar at the College of Nursing, University of Illinois at Chicago (UIC). Her research topic is the comparison of health behavior between Korean elderly and American elderly. (99 words)

6.

Sally Student is a PhD student in the molecular group of Biological Sciences Program at the University of Illinois at Chicago. She holds a Life Sciences B.S. from the National Chung-Hsing University, Taiwan and an Biotechnology M.S. from the University of Pennsylvania. She has been involved in various research projects in the U.S.A. and Taiwan. Her previous research mainly focused on evolution and population genetics. As a first year PhD student, she is pursuing her degree in fundamental genetic research. Ultimately, she would like to strive for permanent cures of diseases, not simply alleviation of illness symptoms. (97 words)

7.

Samantha Student is a PhD candidate in Biochemistry and Molecular Genetics at the University of Illinois at Chicago. She received an MS Degree in Molecular Medicine from the National Cheng Kung University in Taiwan. As a second year PhD student, she and her colleagues presented a mechanism of cell cycle regulated by FoxM1B and this work was published in the *Molecular and Cellular Biology Journal* in 2005. Her research interests are in the field of cancer biology and therapy. Currently, her research mainly focuses on the role of posttranslational modification of FoxM1B in cancerous cells. (93 words)

8.

Serise Student is a Ph.D. medicinal chemistry student at the University of Illinois at Chicago in the College of Pharmacy. She received her B.S. in Biology from Loyola University, Chicago, Illinois, USA. After graduation, she joined Abbott Laboratories for almost ten years as a microbiologist and later as a synthetic organic chemist. In 1998, she received the Scientist of the Year Award at Abbott Laboratories. Her research interest mainly involved infectious diseases. (78 words)

9.

Sandy Student is studying nursing science for a PhD degree at the University of Illinois at Chicago. She holds a Master's and Bachelor's Degree in Nursing Science both from the Catholic University of Korea. She worked as a registered nurse in the university's St. Mary's Hospital for three years. In addition, during her Master's degree in Korea, she worked as a research assistant in the College of Nursing at the Catholic University of Korea for two and half years. (73 words)

10.

Cecelia Student is a Thai graduate student. She worked as a nurse lecturer for fourteen years at Boromrajonani College of Nursing, Nakorn Lampang, Thailand, and her last position was as the academic coordinator of the community health nursing department. She received her bachelor degree in nursing with the silver award from Boromrajonani College of Nursing, Uttaradit, Thailand, and an M.S in Anatomy from the Faculty of Medicine, Chiang Mai University, Thailand. In 2005, she received a scholarship from the Thai Royal Government to study in the United States. Her field of interest is occupational health nursing. (89 words)

11.

Samuel Student is a PhD candidate and teaching assistant in the Department of Electrical Engineering at the University of Illinois at Chicago. His research interests include: signal processing and communication. He received his Bachelor's Degree in Electrical Engineering from Shanghai Jiaotong University, Shanghai, China in 2006. (66 words)

Exercise 2-A, Sample Biostatement

The sample biostatement below was submitted with a manuscript for publication requiring no more than 50 words.

Min Li is currently a GSRA in the Department of Mechanical Engineering and working on the mechanical behaviors of spot welding. He received his BS in physics from ABC University and his MS in mechanical engineering from XYZ University. His major research interests are solid mechanics and spot welding. (49 words)

Please answer the following questions.

1. There are some gaps in Mr. Li's biostatement. What is missing in these gaps?

2. How do you feel about the use of the word *currently*?

3. What is *GSRA*?

4. How do you feel about the chronological order of this biostatement? What type of chronological order should be utilized here?

5. How many research interests does Mr. Li have? How many do you think are appropriate? Is only one good enough? Is five too many? Please discuss.

6. Here are some other items that might appear in a biostatement. Which would you include? Which would you leave out? Why?

Names of journals in which you have been published

Special fellowships or funding

Names of well-known people with whom you have collaborated

7.   Can you think of anything else you would include?

Exercise 2-B, Biostatement Samples (with errors)

Please read and correct the errors.

Stephanie Student received the B.S. degree in nursing from the XYZ University, Seoul, South Korea in 1995 and the M.S. degree in adult nursing from same University in 2001. From 1995 to 2001, she was at the XX Hospital as a nurse and she experienced nursing at the Medical-Surgical ward. From 2001 to 2003 she worked as a researcher and clinical instructor at College of Nursing, the XYZ University and she was responsible for undergraduate student clinical instruction of nephrology, pulmonary, oncology and operation room department. Also, at that time, she published two articles and did oral presentation at two times in the international conference.

Since fall of 2004, she has been in the doctoral program of the College of Nursing XX University. Her department is XX and her research interest is the health promotion of immigrant elderly women.

Exercise 2-C, Biostatement Samples (with errors)

Please read and correct the errors.

Stan Student earned his Bachelor and Master of Engineering at University of XYZ and is currently a full-time MBA student at University of ABC. Before starting MBA study, he ran his own business, small business consulting, in XX for two years. He also worked for a motorcycle trading company as a business control director till 2003. From 1994 to 1999, he worked for XX, which was the world biggest iron steel industrial company, as an engineer. In 1999, he married, resigned his post on, and started his sabbatical for two years. Stan Student graduated from BC University of Economics in 1985 with an honors degree in trade. He then worked as the managers in FG import-export company and DE jewelry company; the latter is the leading jewelry company in AB. During that time Stan Student was also appointed to be the representative of the joint-venture company between CD and the ED company. Stan Student got the Master degree in Economic Development in 1998 taught by the outstanding program between HI and the JK from the Netherlands. Besides business fields, he experienced in education and vocational training. He visited several countries to find different investment environments and capital exchange around the world. He also teaches international business and commercial contracts at the LM University and the College of PQ. He is also the P h. D student at the University of RS since 2004.

Exercise 2-D, Biostatement Samples (with errors)

Please read and correct the errors.

Steven Student is currently a graduate student of chemistry at University of XYZ. He has been involved in several research projects in pharmaceuticals. His research focused mainly on extracting, characterizing, modifying the compounds from aloes, free radicals (nitrogen oxide, super oxygen anion) in signal transduction during innate immune response and photo sensitizer induced tumor cell apoptosis, cyanine dyes delivery in photodynamic therapy, synthesis active pharmaceutical ingredients and antibacterial polymer. He holds a M.S. in biochemistry and molecular science from AB University, PQ, USA and B.S. in chemistry from BC. He has worked in DE Pharmaceutical Company and FG Company. He has been published two papers and applied a patent in JK.

Practice Writing, Bio-statement

Now, it is your turn to write your own bio-statement.

Type a short paragraph of about five sentences describing your schooling since undergraduate years up to the present. (50-60 words)

YOUR NOTES

SECTION 3

Flow

FLOW

Clear writing with good flow steers your reader through the text. Moving from one statement to the next in a smooth fashion adds to the enjoyment of reading. A clear connection of ideas assists your reader's comprehension. We create a nice flow in writing with transitions which are words or phrases that guide the reader.

Exercise 3-A

After reading the following two passages, highlight the parts in sample 2 that differ from sample 1. Why does 2 have better "flow" than 1?

Sample 1

McCormick Tribune Plaza & Ice Rink is a popular site for many Chicagoans and tourists alike. It is situated within Millennium Park just east of Chicago's Loop (business center). December 2001, was the inauguration of this first attraction in Millennium Park; named for the donated funds by the McCormick Tribune Foundation. The ice rink is free to the general public and remains open in the winter from November to March. The area is transformed into Chicago's largest open air dining venue, "Park Grill Plaza" offering beautiful views of Millennium Parks' points of interest and gardens.

Sample 2

Notably, McCormick Tribune Plaza & Ice Rink is a popular site for many Chicagoans and tourists alike. Specifically, it is situated within Millennium Park just east of Chicago's Loop (business center). As a matter of fact, December 2001 was the inauguration of this first attraction in Millennium Park; graciously, named for the donated funds by the McCormick Tribune Foundation. On a daily basis, the ice rink is free to the general public and remains open in the winter from November to March. During the warmer months, the area is transformed into Chicago's largest open air dining venue, "Park Grill Plaza" offering beautiful views of Millennium Parks' points of interest and gardens.

TRANSITION WORDS

To improve your writing, you need to make sure that your ideas, both in sentences and paragraphs, have coherence and are bridged together in a smooth fashion. The use of transitional words and phrases are strongly recommended. This technique brings ideas together in a consistent, logical manner. You may use these words to help continue an idea, designate a shift of thought or contrast, or summarize with a conclusion.

Basic Punctuation Rules When Using Transitions

Look at these examples which demonstrate correct approaches of expressing the same thought:

Robbie studied very hard. However, the teacher still did not like him.

Robbie studied very hard; however, the teacher still did not like him.

Robbie studied very hard. The teacher, however, still did not like him.

Robbie studied very hard. The teacher still did not like him, however.

These transitional words and phrases can assist you in creating a smooth flow to your text.

For continuing a common line of reasoning:

consequently	because
clearly, then	besides that
furthermore	in the same way
additionally	following this further
and	also
in addition	pursuing this further
moreover	in the light of the . . . it is easy to
see that	

To change the line of reasoning (contrast):

however	in contrast	yet
on the other hand	nevertheless	on the contrary
but		

For opening a paragraph initially or for general use:

admittedly	to be sure
assuredly	true
certainly	undoubtedly
granted	unquestionably
no doubt	generally speaking
nobody denies	in general
obviously	at this level
of course	in this situation

For the final points of a paragraph or essay:

finally	to sum up
lastly	to wrap up

Transitional chains, to use in separating sections of a paragraph which is arranged chronologically:

first... second... third...	in the first place
generally... furthermore... finally	just in the same way
in the first place... also... lastly	finally
to be sure... additionally... lastly	
basically...similarly... as well	
in the first place... pursuing this further...finally	

To signal conclusion:

therefore	in conclusion
this	in final consideration
hence	indeed
in final analysis	thus

To restate a point within a paragraph in another way or in a more exacting way:

in other words   specifically
point in fact   pointedly

Sequence or time

after   first...second...third
afterwards   in the first place
as soon as   in the meantime
at first   later
at last   meanwhile
before   next
before long   soon
finally   then

Exercise 3-B, Transitions

Using the previously listed transitions, choose the best transitional word or phrase to complete each sentence. (Hint: sentences 1 – 10 are in chronological order.)

1. _____, you truly love your work.

Admittedly
Moreover
Yet
Therefore
No doubt
Obviously

2._____, your boss and co-workers sense your optimism which inspires them.

  In the final analysis
  Additionally
  Moreover
  Lastly
  In contrast
  Also
  Assuredly

3. Your image as an exemplary employee;_____, may instill jealousy in the office.

  admittedly
  on the other hand
  assuredly
  hence
  yet
  in contrast

4._____, conduct yourself in a humble approach during work.

  Also
  Yet
  In the final analysis
  Lastly
  No doubt
  Therefore

5. Carefully maintain well-balanced office politics, _____.

  finally
  on the other hand
  moreover
  additionally
  to sum up

6. Most employers search for staff members with advanced writing skills, _____ continue reading and writing to sharpen your skills.

    however
    admittedly
    finally
    clearly, then

7. Keep up with new trends in your area of expertise, _____, in your overall business.

    besides this
    likewise
    to illustrate
    what is more
    alternatively

8. The Internet has increased global communication, _____, keep all options open for expansion.

    lastly
    because
    point in fact
    after
    soon

9. _____, webinars have brought employees closer when meeting online.

    This
    Next
    Certainly
    In contrast
    Besides that

10. _____, our company will
announce the initial startup of webinars.

Unquestionably
In final consideration
Moreover
In contrast
True

Transitional Words & Phrases (with exercise)

Additive

1. Addition

    a. To express addition in simple terms

    additionally   in addition to

    moreover   furthermore

    b. To be emphatic

    besides this   what is more

    c. To increase interest of reader

    in fact   actually

    as a matter of fact   indeed

    d. To express different choices

    alternatively   on the other hand

49

2. Exemplification

    a. To exemplify a representative member

        for example   for instance

    b. To exemplify the most important member

        especially   in particular

        particularly   notably

    c. To introduce a specific example which comes in a separate sentence from the preceding general statement

        by way of example   as an illustration

        to illustrate

3. Reference

    To introduce a topic

        considering this

        as for this   concerning this

        regarding this   on the topic/subject of this

        with/in respect to this/the fact that

        with/in regard to this/the fact that

        with/in reference to this/the fact that

4. Similarity

        similarly   in a like manner

        likewise   in the same way   equally

5.   Identification

        namely   specifically   notably   particularly

6.   Clarification

        in other words   so to speak   as one would say

Using Appropriate Transitions

Exercise 3-C

Using the previously listed transitions, fill in the blanks with appropriate transitional words or phrases.

_____, to an ideal geographic location, Nassau,

Bahamas, enjoys a very warm climate. Islands in the Caribbean Ocean possess

beautiful amenities for tourists. _____, St. John and St. Croix

maintain beautiful harbors to launch an excursion upon a seafaring yacht.

_____, scuba diving and snorkeling are world

renowned here among the clear waters and coral reefs.

Adversative Transitions

1. Conflict/Contrast

while	whereas
however	conversely
in contrast	by way of contrast
on the other hand	

2. Concession (Reservation without cancelling the truth of the main clause.)

on the other hand	despite this
however	in spite of this
regardless of this	notwithstanding this
nevertheless	nonetheless
granted this	although, even though, though

3. Dismissal

in either case/event	in any case/event

4. Replacement

rather	instead

Exercise 3-D

Using the transitions listed previously, fill in the blanks with appropriate transitional words or phrases.

_____, the Caribbean islands exude warmth and fun in the sun;

_____, tourists travel to Saint Petersburg, Russia, for much

different reasons. _____, this city is known

for its marvelous architecture. _____of sun tanning on the

beaches, the sightseers spend their days on walking tours in the city.

_____ than packing swim suits and sun tan oil, arrive prepared

with good walking shoes and warm clothing.

_____, enjoy your travels either on land or sea.

Causal Transitions
1.   Cause/Reason

    because, since, as

    due to (the fact that)

    in view of (the fact that)

2.   Effect/Result

    consequently   as a consequence

    thus   hence

    as a result (of this)   in consequence

accordingly   therefore

3.   Condition (all of these are subordinate conjunctions)

if, unless, even if, only if, provided/ing that, granted (that)

Exercise 3-E

Using the transitions listed above, fill in the blanks with appropriate transitional words or phrases.

Tourists must take good care of their health, _____, one

would not want to arrive at the destination in poor health. If one sleeps on the

plane, drinks plenty of water and exercises the legs, _____, "jet

lag" may be avoided. _____ one feels a bit of "jet lag" after

arriving, try to maintain a sensible sleep schedule in the new time zone to

acclimate yourself. _____, in a couple of days one can

adapt to the new schedule like a local.

Sequential Transitions

1.   Beginning

first   initially   to start with

to begin with   first of all

2.   Continuation

previously   next   after this

eventually   subsequently

3.   Conclusion

        finally   at last

        to conclude (with)   as a final point

4.   Digression

        Incidentally

5.   Resumption

        to return to the subject   to resume

6.   Summation

in conclusion	in summary
to summarize	in sum
to sum up	as has been noted/mentioned
as was previously stated	

Exercise 3-F

Using the transitions listed above, fill in the blanks with appropriate transitional words or phrases.

_____, begin with a suitable itinerary for your trip.

_____, search the Internet for fares and lodging,

_____, comparing the cost, convenience, and schedule of the

travel routes. _____, purchase everything,

_____, do not forget to update your passport and

required visas. Bon voyage!

BRIDGING WITH TRANSITIONS

Exercise 3-G

Bridge the two phrases by using an appropriate transition word or phrase from the list on page 57.

Sample:

Chicago winters can be brutally cold and windy; **also,** our temperatures may drop below zero (Fahrenheit).

The Great Lakes greatly affect our wintry weather; _____, the

strong winds cause a wind chill effect. This wind chill factor is colder than the

outside temperature; _____, leading to how we feel this cold air

on our exposed skin due to the wind. One morning, it may be 35 degrees;

_____, by afternoon the temperatures may drop by 20 degrees. Always

dress for the cold in layers ; _____, that way you will be prepared for

changes in weather. Notably, Chicago's winter daytime skies may be crystal

clear with a bright sun shining; _____, the temperatures are

without doubt freezing cold!

For continuing a common line of reasoning:

consequently	clearly, then	besides that
furthermore	in the same way	additionally
following this further		also
in addition	pursuing this further	moreover

To change the line of reasoning (contrast):

however	in contrast	on the other hand	but
yet	nevertheless	on the contrary	

Semicolons (;)

American children have all learned how to use the semicolon in elementary school. Yet, this punctuation mark is not used very often in our writings. Most of us are really not quite sure how to use it! I believe there are significant global differences as to how this punctuation is utilized, so please take note of the American English usage of the semicolon.

- *Use a semicolon in place of a conjunction (and, but, for, or, nor, so, yet) when linking two independent clauses (sentences containing a subject and verb while expressing a complete thought).*

Examples:

1. I will drive to school today; I must go to work after school.

2. It snowed most of the day; by nightfall, we had 7 inches of snow.

3. We baked several different cookies for the children; they did not eat very many.

(The sample sentences are also referred to as compound sentences since each independent clause is made up of its own subject, verb, and object.)

Exercise 3-H

Match two independent clauses to create a compound sentence linked together with a semicolon.

1. Aaron made his bed   _____the class is scheduled for 4 PM on Tuesdays

2. your e-mail account is not working   _____he proceeded to get dressed

3. it is located on the third floor of the library   _____I do not know what the problem could be

4. our bus was late   _____it's such a beautiful sunny day

5. let's go swimming at the beach   _____everyone was late to work

6. traffic is backed up from the rain   _____we decided to walk to school

In this space write the sentences with the correct clauses (do not forget about punctuation).

_____

_____

_____

_____

_____

- **You may use a semicolon when a transitional word or phrase is placed in the middle of a sentence creating two independent clauses. Always remember to follow that transition with a comma.**

Examples:

I was early for class today; therefore, I took advantage of the extra time and studied.

Class was dismissed early this afternoon; nonetheless, we covered all the material scheduled.

My chosen course of study is quite challenging; for that reason, most of my classmates have formed study groups.

- **Do not use a semicolon in place of a comma, dash, or colon.**

- **The semicolon is used to separate phrases of items in a series.**

  The annual convention has members traveling from Chicago, Illinois; Miami, Florida; Denver, Colorado; and Boston, Massachusetts.

- **The semicolon is used to separate units in a series when one or more of those units contain commas.**

  We all brought camping equipment to the site: pots, pans, silverware, cups, plates; coffee, bread, meat, fruit, vegetables; tents, sleeping bags, flashlights, matches; and candy, popcorn, chewing gum, cookies.

Exercise 3-1

Now, it's your turn to write three sentences using the semicolon appropriately.

_____

_____

_____

REDUCING WORDINESS

Contrary to writing methods you may have previously learned, American academic writing is neither flowery, nor wordy. We strive for concise text in a straight forward manner. Of course, this holds true for non-fiction writing. If and when you are asked to compose fiction, then you may have free reign with as many descriptive words you deem necessary.

In order to train yourself in this method of succinct writing, begin by free writing your paragraphs without worry of specific wording, punctuation, and spelling. Then, go back and proofread (read what you already have written) out loud to listen and read for potential modifications to tighten up the wording. By reading aloud, you are able to review your own writing using two strategies which are quite helpful. At your level of education, proofreading is essential before submitting any written work.

First, one method of selecting replacement words, and at the same time increasing your vocabulary, is by right clicking with the mouse on a given word when working in Word software. A drop-down menu will appear, click on *synonyms,* and a list of words with similar meanings will come into view. Easily replace the word by double clicking on your selection.

Second, you may reduce wordiness and continue smooth flow by replacing nouns in subsequent sentences with demonstrative pronouns (this & these for close proximity and that & those for further proximity). This is another method of continuing good flow without the use of transitions.

Examples:

> An academic job may be complex to secure since more students are choosing to attend graduate school. *This* results in a very competitive job market.

> *This* refers to job in the first sentence.

> Academia offers much more than teaching and *those* jobs range from advisors, research, administration and student affairs just to name a few.

> *Those* refer to academia in the first part of the sentence.

Demonstrative Pronouns + Explanatory Nouns

These demonstrative pronouns are to be used after the subject noun has already been mentioned.

this (singular, close in distance)   these (plural, close in distance)

that (singular, far in distance)   those (plural, far in distance)

When we team these pronouns with explanatory nouns, we can continue discussing the subject in subsequent sentences without being redundant.

A number of academic writing explanatory nouns:

method	feature	aspect	dilemma
characteristic	explanation	motive	effect
outcome	condition	fact	trend

For example: All good <u>men</u> and <u>women</u> must come to the aid of children. <u>These characteristics</u> are commendable.

Our science <u>research</u> was reported in last year's journal. <u>Those methods</u> have become standard procedure in many labs throughout the country.

Here, one may think that the writing is becoming redundant; but no, the writer is highlighting previously mentioned information in a different style that lends to the overall flow of the paper.

Third, other situations that may lead to wordiness are translating from your native language to English; grammar problems; unsure of word forms; and lack of vocabulary.

The children *are very easy to* jump rope.   (Direct translation from native language and unfamiliar with adverbial word forms.)

CORRECT: The children jump rope *easily.*

By riding the train downtown, *it* will save money.   (Grammar problems and student not using gerund as subject.)

CORRECT: *Riding* the train downtown saves money.

When children *are bad,* they talk *in a bad way.*   (Word form problem, student using wordy prepositional phrase since he/she does not know adverb form.)

CORRECT: When children *misbehave*, they talk *rudely*.

Last night, the little girl *was the center of attention*.   (Vocabulary problem.)

CORRECT: Last night, everyone *focused* on the little girl.

Exercise 3-J

After carefully reviewing the previous page 62, choose a noun to complete each sentence.

1. The campus is quiet now during winter break, but spring semester will soon begin and more than 25,000 students will converge onto the university grounds. This _____ livens up the area.

     solitude   transformation   calm

2. Most everyone has already registered before the first day of class, but there are always latecomers for one reason or another. These _____ can cause disruptions in teaching time.

     situations   strategies   inspirations

3. Scheduling a full-time semester of classes can be an overwhelming task at first. Yet, looking back on my own college days, those _____ became an interesting puzzle to solve.

     times   lectures   results

4. Last semester's first day of class was full of eager students' optimism and unbridled energy. That UIC _____ fueled the university toward an extremely successful academic year.

market   enthusiasm   work

As you can see, these nouns preceded with demonstrative pronouns (this, that, these, those) refer back to what you have expressed in the first sentence. Thus, you have learned how to summarize the same idea in fewer words.

Expressive Vocabulary

Another method to bring conciseness to your writing is by using strong expressive vocabulary; whereby, eliminating vague non-specific descriptions. Take note of the following examples.

WORDY: We *had a great time* with many people at the party *to close out the year of 2011 and begin the new year of 2012.* (25 words)
CONCISE: We *celebrated* with many people at a *2012 New Year's Eve party.* (12 words)

WORDY: Sam *was always aware of all the people who worked for him* and *their feelings* when *giving them directions at work* as their manager. (24 words)
CONCISE: As manager, Sam *was compassionate* when *training employees at work.* (10 words)

WORDY: Learning a second language can be *quite difficult and a lot of trouble* at times; especially, when studying *in another country.* (21 words)
CONCISE: Learning a second language can be a *disadvantage* at times; especially, when studying *abroad.* (14 words)

WORDY: *At the end of the eight hour work shift that finished at 5 PM, people got in their cars to drive home as others walked or rode their bicycles away.* **(30 words)**

CONCISE: *By 5 PM, the end of the work day, people disappeared toward home.* **(13 words)**

YOUR NOTES

SECTION 4

Sentence Level

Definitions

NOUNS

Proper nouns which name people, places or things in English are always capitalized with the first letter. The names of cities, states, countries, oceans, rivers, mountain ranges, historical sites, companies, and peoples' names are but a few examples of ***proper nouns***. ***Proper nouns*** name specific items. For instance:

McDonalds	Chicago	Illinois	Shanghai
China	Italy	Atlantic Ocean	
Mississippi River	Himalayas	Mary Jones	Great Wall
Taj Mahal	White House		

At times, it is necessary to use "the" before certain proper nouns. If a country is made up of several parts, (as in: **the** United States of America, **the** United Kingdom, **the** Republic of Lebanon).

states	the United States, the United States of America, the USA, the US
kingdom	the United Kingdom, the UK, the Kingdom of Saudi Arabia
republic	the French Republic, the People's Republic of China, the Republic of Philippines, the Republic of the Congo, the Republic of Lithuania, the Republic of Singapore

All other nouns are called **common nouns,** which also name people, places or things. These are different from proper nouns since they name general items. **Common nouns** are not capitalized with the first letter unless they begin a sentence or are in a title. For instance:

Common Nouns	Proper Nouns
continent	Africa
computer company	IBM
automobile	Volvo
store	Target
book	Webster's Dictionary

Exercise 4-A

Please read the following paragraph and correct the noun capitalization errors.

paul wanted to take an automobile trip through the united states appalachian

mountains, so he and his brother began making plans on his dell computer.

they routed their journey from chicago, illinois, east through indiana and began

their mountain climbing in kentucky. tennessee was the next state to hike;

meandering their way toward north carolina's beautiful mountaintop ranges.

once they reached the state of virginia, paul was complaining of sore feet. Yet,

the two brothers were able to complete their journey by enjoying the mountain

peaks of the maryland appalachians.

Articles

Every single, **<u>countable</u>** noun in English requires an article: ***a, an***, or ***the***.

Following are some rules for the definite article ***the***.

1. If the noun has been earlier identified.

    > I bought a Ford automobile. It's the first automobile I have ever bought.

2. If the noun is unique.

    > the sun, the moon, the weather, the king, the president, the pope,
    >
    > the world, etc.

3. If the noun is specific. (These are often followed by prepositional phrases or relative clauses.)

    > The student next to me was sleeping in his seat.
    >
    > The cup of coffee that I just drank was too hot.

4. If an adjective is being used like a noun.

    > The humble seem confident in their ways.
    >
    > America offers many supportive programs for the poor.

5. If there is a superlative, ordinal number, or year.

    > the best, the worst, the sixth one, the eighth eldest daughter

6. If there is "of" in a name. (typically)

    The Republic of Korea

    The Bank of Hong Kong

    The University of Illinois at Chicago

7. With certain adjectives indicating a time sequence.

    the beginning, the middle, the end, the next, the following, etc.

8. With canals, deserts, forests, oceans, rivers, and seas.

The Suez Canal	The Sahara Desert
The Black Forest	The Pacific Ocean
The Mississippi River	The South China Sea

9. With islands, lakes and mountains when they are plural, not singular.

The Canary Islands	but	Vancouver Island
The Great Lakes	but	Lake Michigan
The Rocky Mountains	but	Mount Fuji

10. Names of theories, effects, devices, scales, etc., modified by a proper name and used as an adjective. If the proper name is used in possessive form, then no article is necessary.

The Fourier transform	but	Einstein's theory of relativity
The Doppler effect	but	Broca's area
The Hubble telescope	but	Wegener's hypothesis
The Fahrenheit scale	but	Newton's laws of motion

Following are some rules for the indefinite article *a & an*. This indefinite article is used for non-specific nouns or any member of a given group.

1. The indefinite article *a* is used before any unspecific noun that begins with a consonant *sound* even when spelled with a vowel. *A euro is the form of several European countries' money. (The word euro begins with the vowel e, but it is pronounced with the beginning sound of the consonant y. Therefore, it requires the article* **a**.)

2. The indefinite article *an* is used before any unspecific noun that begins with a vowel *sound* even when spelled with a consonant. *An honorary grant was awarded to the English professor. (The word honorary begins with the consonant h, but it is pronounced with the beginning sound of the vowel o. Therefore, it requires the article* **an**.)

Exercise 4-B

Please fill in the blanks with a, an, the, or 0 or insert articles where necessary.

The ever popular American jeans were crafted by two immigrants in ____ latter

part of ____ 19th century. Originally, Jacob Davis and Levi Strauss designed this

rugged wear for ____ farm hands who worked ____ land from sun-up to sun-

down. Denim fabric proved to withstand ____ brutal work these pants were

subjected to on ____ regular basis. "Waist overalls" were ____ original name for

these pants, and it was not until ____ 1960s when the "baby boomer generation"

made them popular and began calling them blue jeans. Today around ____

world, one can find jeans in style just about anywhere.

Exercise 4-C

Please fill in the blanks with the articles: a, an, the, or 0 if nothing is required.

Skateboarding has developed over ____ last sixty-odd years into____very popular

sport throughout ____ U.S.A. It all began in California when surfers decided to

bring their sport to ____ streets. Initially, they attempted simple construction

with____smaller wooden surfboard along with front and back roller skates. As

the surfers navigated ____street's pavement while having fun, they continued to

improve upon ____ design of their original model. During ____early years of

skateboarding, experimentation ruled ____ sport from its infancy. Eventually,

____boards and wheels were highly refined into ____ ever popular skateboards

we see today.

Generic Nouns

A generic noun or noun phrase can represent an entire class or be one
representative of a class of objects, people, quantities, or ideas. Look at this
example.

*The computer has essentially transformed our global efficiency in a multitude of
areas.*

In this example, *computer* is not a specific machine. It is a generic noun that
represents the entire class of computers. It is important to know how to use
articles with generic nouns for these reasons:

1.   They often occur in highly formal, academic English.

2.   They often occur in introductions and conclusions because they are closely
     associated with generalizations.

3.   They often occur in initial sentences in paragraphs.

4.   They often are subjects in sentences.

<u>Specific vs. Generic Nouns</u>

Please look at these examples.

<u>Specific</u>

The electric car engineered by the Italian team won the prize.

The computer crashed after I worked for 12 hours non-stop yesterday.

Add some water to the recipe.

The trees in rural areas grow rapidly.

<u>Generic</u>

The electric car will become reality for production soon.

The computer has replaced the typewriter.

Water is vital for all living things.

Trees are imperative to our environment to control temperatures and wind.

<u>Abstract vs. Concrete Generic Nouns</u>

Another feature that is very difficult to make is the difference between abstract and concrete generic nouns. Abstract generics refer to *an entire class* while concrete generics refer to *a representative of the class*. Please look at these examples.

<u>Abstract Generic</u>

The killer bee subsists widespread in Mexico.

<u>Concrete Generic</u>

A killer bee pursues perceived threats far from its hive.

Killer bees are more defensive than their European counterparts.

The laser has modernized surgery.

A laser may be used by an ophthalmologist to treat cataracts.

The computer has replaced the typewriter.

Computers are essential to university studies.

Advice for different disciplines

Formal, academic English generally favors the abstract generic (i.e., the computer….). In the hard sciences (e.g., electrical engineering, physics, etc.), the concrete plural generic is favored (i.e., computers…..). In medicine, body parts almost always are preceded by *the*, diseases are almost always preceded by *a* or nothing, and proper nouns used as adjectives are almost always possessive. Look at these examples.

Body parts	*Diseases/Conditions*	*Names with diseases*
the liver	a cold	Lou Gehrig's disease
the heart	a heart attack	Tourette's syndrome
the kidneys	cancer	Meniere's disease
	influenza (the flu)*	

While reading journal articles in your subject area, make note of how the authors present generic nouns; in order to, garner helpful lessons from the experienced writers.

General to Specific Writing

Graduate writing quite often begins with an introductory remark that is general in nature and then proceeds to more specific text. Our educational system has groomed us in producing assignments in this format. A general to specific answer is suitable for:

- an examination question
- an introductory paragraph
- setting the stage for a background paragraph of an analysis or discussion

Writing in the general to specific format as a rule begins with one of the following:

- a brief or expanded definition,
- a definition that compares or contrasts,
- a statement of purpose or generalization, or
- a statement of fact.

The text progresses from a wide, general proclamation to more specific sentences. At times, the statements can become quite broad toward the conclusion.

G E N E R A L

SPECIFIC

MORE PRECISE

C O N C L U S I O N

SENTENCE LEVEL DEFINITIONS

A sentence level definition is simply one sentence that defines your topic. That topic may be your field of study, a hobby that interests you, a political and/or religious stance, or your opinion on something. Later, we will expand this sentence level definition into a paragraph level definition.

SAMPLES:

A **microbe** presents itself as a microorganism, in particular a pathogenic bacterium.

A **holistic** approach to medicine is a system of treatments, principally those considered outside normal scientific medicine, as natural or chiropractic; often considering nutritional measures: *holistic medicine*.

Stocks are company/corporation shares offered publicly on the stock market.

An **android** is a robotic machine.

Liabilities are moneys to be paid to the lender.

Hedge is the prevention of a complete loss of a bet, disagreement, or investment, with a partly counterbalancing or qualifying one.

Marketing is transferring merchandise from the seller to buyer, plus advertising, transport, storage, and selling.

GDP (gross domestic product) is the entire value of all goods and services produced domestically by one nation during a year.

Economics is the study of production, distribution, and consumption of goods and services, or the material interests of humanity.

French is a romance language spoken in France, areas of Belgium and Switzerland; colonized regions by France, as well.

Geology is the science of physical history of the earth, rocks of which it is composed, and physical, chemical, and biological changes (past and present) the earth has experienced.

A gerontological nurse practitioner is a registered nurse with a master's degree from a nurse practitioner program specializing in the care of older adults, who can diagnose and manage acute and chronic diseases while taking a holistic approach to older people's needs.

Neuroprosthesis integrates the nervous system with electrical or mechanical devices to correct or supplement a damaged neurological function.

Philosophy is the study, based on reason, of the truths and principles of being, knowledge, or conduct.

DEFINITIONS

A frequent method of starting a paper is with a sentence definition, beginning with a general description and proceeding on to more specifics on the topic. Considering that your audience is learned with the subject area, this definition will reveal your comprehension of the given theories.

CREATING A DEFINITION

A word's meaning is explained in a definition. In our English language, a single word may have more than one meaning dependent upon the context.

Additionally, words or phrases may have different meanings depending on the field of study. For example, *tone* has several definitions. In music, a *tone* can be a sound of distinct pitch, quality, and duration; while in linguistics, *tone* can refer to the rise or fall of the voice on a particular syllable (as in Chinese). In interior design, *tone* may be a color or shade of color. Finally, *tone* in physiology may be used to describe the normal state of elastic tension or partial contraction in resting muscles.

Exercise 4-D

Writing a Sentence Level Definition Exercise

Write a **one-sentence** definition for one of the following terms. Make sure you provide enough specific detail to distinguish your term from other members of the class.

a bridge	a computer virus	a laser
a conductor	a carcinogen (cancer causing agent)	a mentor/advisor
a piano	a landfill (buried trash)	a residence hall or dormitory

_____

_____

_____

Relative Clauses

To review, a relative clause describes a noun or pronoun. For instance,

noun   *relative clause describing teacher*

The teacher, **who missed class yesterday,...**

pronoun   *relative clause describing he*

He, **who does not study for exams,...**

Reduced Relative Clauses

The distinguishing information in the second part of a sentence-level definition can be introduced by either a full or reduced relative clause. Reduced relative clauses are often preferred in academic writing because they are more concise.

Relative clauses may be reduced if:

1. the relative clause consists only of the relative pronoun, a form of *to be*, and one or more prepositional phrases

    - *Enamel is a rigid, white inorganic substance that is on the crown of each tooth.*

    - *Enamel is a rigid, white inorganic substance on the crown of each tooth.*

    ➤ *A gill is an external respiratory organ which is at the rear of the mouth of most aquatic animals.*

    ➤ *A gill is an external respiratory organ at the rear of the mouth of most aquatic animals.*

2. the relative clause consists of a passive verb plus some *additional information*

    - *A theater is a constructed building which has been purposely intended for theatrical presentations.*

    - *A theater is a constructed building purposely intended for theatrical presentations.*

    ➤ *Human hair visible to the eye is the hair shaft, which has gone dormant.*

    ➤ *Human hair visible to the eye is the hair shaft considered dormant.*

3.   the relative clause contains the relative pronoun, an adjective ending in *–ble*, plus *additional information*

   - *A robot is a programmable machine which is capable of performing the work of a human.*

   - *A robot is a programmable machine capable of performing the work of a human.*

4.   the relative clause contains the verb *have*. Eliminate the relative pronoun and the verb *have*. They can be replaced by the word *with*.

   - *Parliament is a national governing body which has the highest level of legislative authority within a state.*

   - *Parliament is a national governing body with the highest level of legislative authority within a state.*

5.   the relative clause contains an active state verb (not *to be* or *have*). The relative pronoun is dropped and the verb is changed to the *–ing* form.

   - *Pollution is a form of contamination that often results from human being activity.*

   - *Pollution is a form of contamination often resulting from human being activity.*

   ➢ *A moon is a natural satellite which orbits around a planet.*

   ➢ *A moon is a natural satellite orbiting around a planet.*

Relative clauses may NOT be reduced if:

1.   there is a modal auxiliary in the clause. (Modals are helping verbs expressing time and mood, i.e., can, must, should, would.)

- The government agency that *must* monitor the production of all American food is the Food and Drug Administration.

2.   there is a preposition before the pronoun *which*.

- A foundation is a base *on which* a constructed building is erected.

Stylistic advice

1.   Do NOT end your clause with a preposition or particle (short words, such as articles, conjunctions, and negatives).

- A foundation is a base where a structure is *built on*. **NOT GOOD**

2.   Use *whereby* instead of *by which*, *by means of which*, and *through which*.

- Collective bargaining is a method *whereby* employers agree to converse about work-related issues with employee representatives.

3.   Avoid *when* and *where* in formal definitions.

- Pollution is *when* the environment becomes tainted as a result of human activity. **NOT ADVISED!**

- Pollution is a form of environmental contamination resulting from human activity. **GOOD**

- A fault is *where* there is a fracture in the earth's crust and the rock on one side of the fracture shifts in relation to the rock on the other side. ***NOT ADVISED!***

- A fault is a fracture in the earth's crust *in which* the rock on one side of the fracture shifts in relation to the rock on the other side. ***GOOD***

4. Avoid using any form of the term in your definition.

- Erosion is a process during which the exterior of the earth *erodes*. ***NOT ADVISED!***

- Erosion is a process during which the exterior of the earth is degraded by the effects of the atmosphere, weather, and human activity. ***GOOD***

Exercise 4-E

Reduced Relative Clause Activity

Please reduce the sentences, if possible.

1. A catalyst is a substance that can speed up the rate of a chemical reaction without changing its own structure.

2. A black hole is a celestial body which has approximately the same mass as the sun and a gravitational radius of about 3 km.

3. Heat is a form of energy which can be transmitted through solid and liquid media by conduction.

4. A brake is a device that is capable of slowing the motion of a mechanism.

5. A dome is generally a hemispherical roof which is on top of a circular, square, or other-shaped structure.

6. A piccolo is a small flute that is pitched an octave higher than a standard flute.

Exercise 4-F

Complete the following sentences by inserting the appropriate preposition (by, on, in, of).

1. A thermometer is an instrument _____ which temperature can be measured.

2. Photosynthesis is a process _____ which sunlight is used to manufacture carbohydrates from water and carbon dioxide.

3. A credit bureau is an organization _____ which businesses can apply for financial information on potential customers.

4. An anhydride is a compound _____ which the elements of water have been removed.

5. An eclipse is a celestial event _____ which one body, such as a star, is covered by another, such as a planet.

6. An axis is an imaginary line _____ which a body is said to rotate.

Exercise 4-G

Please reduce the following *if possible grammatically or stylistically*.

1. Section 6 is devoted to numerical examples that demonstrate the necessity of the line source models.

2. Chinatown is a tourist attraction that serves as an introduction to Chinese culture and cuisine for other residents of the city.

3. It is suggested that one of the principal challenges facing public health professionals is to determine the factors that influence, facilitate, and then maintain exercise participation in a majority of the older population.

4. Sixteen Chinese restaurant owners/managers will be selected randomly from a list which will be provided by the Chinatown Chamber of Commerce.

5. The proportion of older individuals who participate regularly in physical activity is disappointingly low.

6. Two studies noted that in areas where there was a high prevalence of HIV, male circumcision was not traditionally practiced.

Practice Writing

Now, it is your turn to write a sentence level definition from your field of study.

Write only one sentence.

YOUR NOTES

SECTION 5

Paragraph Level

Definitions

Student X
Course #
Paragraph Level Definition
Date

SAMPLE OF A PARAGRAPH LEVEL DEFINITION

Title: **Risk Factors for Childhood Obesity**

Topic sentence:
    Childhood obesity is a worldwide problem. There are many factors associated with our youth's problem in gaining weight uncontrollably.

Support 1:
    Significantly, three major aspects influence childhood obesity: genetics, inadequate physical activity, and unhealthy eating behavior.

Support 2:
    Additionally, being overweight has a significant influence on one's health. Youngsters who are overweight and obese are more likely to have an abnormal glucose tolerance, as well as, high cholesterol and blood pressure values.

Support 3:
    The increase of childhood obesity has raised concerns about these individual's healthy status since obesity is associated with physical, psychological, and social health problems.

Concluding sentence:
    In conclusion, increasing children's physical activity and promoting healthy eating habits can help maintain desired body weight while preventing obesity.

Student X
Course #
Paragraph Level Definition
Date

Risk Factors for Childhood Obesity

Childhood obesity is a worldwide problem. There are many factors associated with our youth's dilemma in gaining weight uncontrollably. Significantly, three major aspects influence childhood obesity: genetics, inadequate physical activity, and unhealthy eating behavior. Additionally, being overweight has a significant influence on one's health. Youngsters who are overweight and obese are more likely to have an abnormal glucose tolerance, as well as, high cholesterol and blood pressure values. The increase of childhood obesity has raised concerns about these individual's health status since obesity is associated with physical, psychological, and social health problems. In conclusion, increasing children's physical activity and promoting healthy eating habits can help maintain desired body weight while preventing obesity.

Exercise 5–A

Extended Definition Paragraphs

Read the following extended definition; answer the questions:

Navigation is a process by which means of transport can be guided to their destination when the route has few or no landmarks. Some of the earliest navigators were sailors, who steered their ships first by the stars, then with a compass, and later with more complicated instruments that measured the position of the sun. We are reminded of this by the fact that the word *navigation* comes from the Latin word for "ship." However, the history and importance of navigation changed radically in the twentieth century with the development of aircraft and missiles which fly in three dimensions. Today, both ships and aircraft rely heavily on computerized navigational systems that can provide a continuous, immediate, and accurate report of position.

1. What type of information is included in each of the sentences in the definitions?

2. How is the passage organized?

3. What verb tenses are used for which sentences? Why?

4. Sentence three begins with *we*. Is this appropriate?

Notice how the paragraph moves from a very general statement at the beginning to specific details, then "widens out" again in the final sentence to describe the current status of navigation. This pattern is quite common in paragraphs of this type.

Exercise 5-B

This is an example of a general to specific paragraph:

[1]Pollution is a form of ecological contamination consequential to human activity.

[2]Specifically, some common types of pollution are waste from the burning of

fossil fuels. [3]Additionally, factory sewage and toxic chemicals can enter our

waterways, resulting in polluted water. [4]Even litter and excessive noise can be

considered forms of pollution because of the impact they can have on the

environment. [5]The pollution problem can and will be resolved to clean up our

environment.

List the general sentences and specific sentence/s.

General Sentences   **Specific Sentences**

GENERALIZATIONS

Up to now, our focus has been on beginning general to specific passages with definitions. Certainly, one may choose alternate methods. As well, a generalization based on facts may be the way to commence with your writing. If you are presented with an assignment to write on the American Civil War, you may write your opening sentence as a definition.

> ***The United States Civil War, also referred to as the War between the States, was fought from April 1861 until April 1865.***

Nevertheless, an alternate introduction would be to establish a topic sentence with a generalization.

> ***The United States Civil War was fought between the northern and southern states over the basic issue of slavery in the late 1800s.***

The preference is yours for the choosing, yet your topic may work better with one choice rather than the other.

After opening with a general sentence, your subsequent sentences present support in more specific terms.

Exercise 5-C

Sentence Sequencing

Number 1 through 7 in logical order, general to specific, creating one paragraph.

The Internet

_____ In the not too distant past, we marveled at how TV phenomenally connected us with others so far away, but people are enjoying this new technology in novel forms of contact.

_____ The Internet has expanded our horizons in astounding ways that affect the world's population.

_____ Our future will reveal Internet wonders beyond our imagination.

_____ This effect is bringing people closer than ever before through travel and the World Wide Web.

_____ Communication has been streamlined with data packages that allow one to connect by cell phone, texting, and social media which may lead to a whole other topic of romance.

_____ For instance, no longer will you need to go shopping for an engagement ring at the jewelry store downtown, when online shopping is so much more convenient.

_____ Dating online has redefined the whole meaning of meeting someone with common interests, developing a meaningful relationship, and perhaps making a commitment.

Correct Order of Paragraph Sentences

Exercise 5-D

Put the following sentences in the correct order for a general to specific extended definition.

Palindromes

_____ The term itself comes from the ancient Greek word *palindromos* meaning "running back again".

_____ Another good and more recent example is "If I had a Hi-Fi."

_____ Some very common English words are palindromes, such as *pop*, *dad*, and *noon*.

_____ A palindrome is a word or phrase that results in the same sequence of letters whether it is read from left to right or from right to left.

_____ One of the classic long palindromes is "A man, a plan, a canal, Panama."

_____ Long palindromes are very hard to construct, and some word puzzlers spend immense amounts of time trying to produce good examples.

Comparative Extended Definitions

Extended definitions usually begin with a general, one-sentence definition and then become more specific as additional details are provided. Extended definitions need to display one or more of the following.

1. Analysis of components/elements   (what composes the thing you are describing)

2. Knowledge of applications   (how something works or is used)

3. Exemplification   (giving examples of what it is you are defining)

4. Historical change and development

5. Future prediction

Exercise 5-E

Please read the following definitions and decide which of the above characteristics they display. They may contain more than one characteristic but decide which one is the primary focus.

1. computer   Also called a processor. Electronic piece of equipment that recognizes information, executes certain mathematical and logical functions very quickly, and exhibits these functions' results.

2. university   An institution of the highest level of learning, maintaining a liberal arts college and graduate studies program along with several professional schools and certified to award undergraduate and graduate degrees.

3. screen saver   A program displaying an image on a computer monitor avoiding a still image from "burning" into the screen's phosphor. These generally begin automatically after no activity for a fixed time.

4. viking   Scandinavian pirates who plundered Europe's seacoasts during the 8th to 10th centuries as thieves.

5. software   *Programs directing computer operations (laptops, cell phones, robotics, tablets), plus instructional documents on how to use them.*

6. advertising   Calling public attention to a product, service, need, etc., particularly by paid announcements in print; radio or TV; billboards; etc., in order to acquire more customers.

Exercise 5-F

Paragraph Level Definitions

After reading this paragraph's topic and concluding sentences, compose three support sentences in the paragraph's body.

America's International Students

(General) Topic sentence: Year after year, international students are increasing their numbers at American universities ready to gain knowledge from a broad range of disciplines.

(Specific) Support #1:

(Specific) Support #2:

(Specific) Support #3:

(General) Concluding sentence: Our college campuses are becoming havens of diversity; contributing to truth in the term, "It's a small world after all!"

Exercise 5-G

After reading this paragraph's four supportive sentences, compose a topic and concluding sentence.

(General) Topic sentence:

(Specific) Support #1: The Eastern Seaboard is comprised of the original New England states lying just south of the northeasterly dense forests and majestic mountains extending to the Canadian border.

(Specific) Support #2: As for our southern states, they reflect charming genteel manners and friendly hospitality in a slower pace; in fact, their deeply rooted family convictions, along with distinctive cuisine and style of music, conjure up home-sweet-home feelings.

(Specific) Support #3: The Midwest is often referred to as America's heartland of fertile agricultural area where land varies from great flat plains to small rolling hills; good traditional family values and hard work ethics prevail.

(Specific) Support #4 The American West comprises over one-half the land area of the country where the diverse terrain ranges from mountains, forests, deserts, and fertile valleys; western cowboys settled the "wild west," worked the land and set up towns for new settlers.

(General) Concluding sentence:

Practice Writing

Now, it is your turn to write a paragraph level definition.

Type a 5 sentence paragraph as a paragraph level definition. Your topic sentence will begin with the sentence level definition you have already written. Keep in mind, the general to specific format. Your first sentence is general; sentences 2, 3, and 4 are more specific in supporting your topic. The 5th and last sentence is your conclusion, wherein, you may return to a generalization or future prediction.

SECTION 6

Data
Commentaries

Writing Data Commentaries

Your graduate studies will most likely solicit you to comment on illustrated graphs, figures, and/or tables. This data may have been authored by another, or perhaps it stems from your own research and results. As you are creating a professional image within your own discipline, here is an opportunity to present comments in the accepted manner. Such illustrations can be easily read; therefore, simply describing the image would be a disservice to your audience. Additionally, be careful not to demean your readers' comprehension. Your job here is not to describe the depicted data, but to make observational statements from general to more specific trends. Always keep in mind to use the appropriate strength of claim as not to offend any authors.

Hedging Exercise (Hedging is to be cautious, evade an issue in a polite way.)

In order to practice using terminology to comment on data, the following vocabulary is suggested.

verbs	suggest, seem, tend, appear to be, believe, think, doubt, indicate, assume, contribute to, cause
modal verbs	must, would, will, might, may, could
adverbs	probably, most likely, often, at times, usually, certainly, definitely, clearly, possibly, perhaps, conceivably

Exercise 6-A

Rank letters *a* through *f* according to the strongest claim (1) to the weakest claim (7).

Unstable study habits_____ poor grades at the end of the semester.

a. may have caused   _____ 5
b. contributed to   _____ 2
c. were one cause of   _____ 4
d. caused   _____ 1
e. might have contributed   _____ 6
f. most likely caused   _____ 3
g. could have caused   _____ 7

Your context will determine the correct choice.

Data comments may focus on one or more of these intentions.

❖ Discuss data suggestions

❖ Compare diverse data

❖ Highlight results

❖ Evaluate theories, practices, or beliefs per specified data

❖ Evaluate data consistency as regards the methodology utilized

Your review of the statistics will most likely take into account no less than three of these above.

Structure of Data Comments

Data comments are often broken up into two sections. These are *discussion* and *results.*

Discussion

The discussion section offers a dialogue on the *analysis* and *implications* of the data. Instead of just writing up what occurred or what is revealed through the graphics, you begin to interpret the data into your own words, **in the present tense.**

Whereas it may be….   =   implications and analysis

As for using 1st (I, we) or 3rd person (singular: he, she, it & plural: they), some disciplines allow for 1st person if you have gathered the data and are writing about what you have done. However, in general, you really do want to focus on the data. For that reason, most data commentaries are in 3rd person.

IMPORTANT: Most authors tend to write their data commentaries' **discussion sections in the present verb tense.** Whereby, **results' sections are usually written in the past tense.** Peruse various discipline explicit journals in your major field of study to observe how your colleagues are writing their articles.

Results

The results section should have these elements.

1.   Location identifier

2.   Summary statement

3.   Highlights of interest

The results section is **frequently written in the *past tense*** because you are commenting on data collection that took place in the past. Nonetheless, you will also see results written in the *present* or *present perfect tense* if you are treating the data as common truth; wherein, it holds true for today.

Table F-1....	=	is the location
shows the.....	=	summary statement (present tense)
As can be seen	=	linking *as* clause
the greatest....	=	highlight #1
At the same time,	=	transition (connecting) word
it is amazing.....	=	highlight #2

Data Commentary Verb Tenses

DISCUSSION SECTION	RESULTS SECTION
present tense (interpret data)	past tense (data collected in past)
	present tense (holds true today)
	present perfect tense (holds true today)

DATA COMMENTARIES

Review of linking "as clauses"

These clauses are very useful in giving information about data from a graph,

table, or figure.

examples: *As shown in Table 5,* home disks are the most frequent
source of infection.

As can be seen in Figure 8, infant mortality is still high in
third world countries.

As revealed by the graph, the defect rate is continuing to
decline.

HIGHLIGHTING STATEMENTS

Highlighting statements are generalizations that you have drawn from the
data.

Do <u>not</u> simply repeat the details, attempt to cover all of the information,
or claim more than is reasonable or defensible.

The ways of qualifying or moderating a claim that you have highlighted are
always done with caution and use of modals for probability. (You do not
want to make statements that are definitive.)

examples: (probability)

A reducing diet *will result in* a loss of weight.

A reducing diet *may result in* a loss of weight.

A reducing diet *might/could result in* a loss of weight.

(Other words to imply probability: *almost certain, probable, likely, possible, &*
unlikely.)

Also, distance your statements with soft expressions to maintain your
generalizations. (i.e.: have, seem, appear)

examples: (distancing)

Economists *have less* assurance in global stability since the recession.

Economists *seem to have less* assurance in global stability since the recession.

Economists *appear to have less* assurance in global stability since the recession.

It would seem that economists have less assurance in global stability since the
recession.

Beginning with transitional phrases:

On the boundless information available,

In the view of an authority on the subject,

According to this prelude to the research,

Based on various interpretations already made,

Another way to defend a generalization is to qualify the subject.

examples: (qualifying the subject)

Many economists have less assurance in global stability since the recession.

A majority of economists have less assurance in global stability since the recession.

In most parts of the country, economists have less assurance in global stability since the recession.

Economists, *in most declining markets,* have less assurance in global stability since the recession.

Lastly, exceptions may be added and weaker verbs substituted for strong verbs.

examples:

> *With the exception of*
>
> *Apart from*
>
> *Except for*

Strong Verbs	Weaker Verbs
establish	**set up**

Private schools were established/set up at the request of many parents.

appoint	**suggest**

Members of the Board of Trustees were appointed/suggested by the local government.

change	**adjust**

The international student changed/adjusted his schedule to accommodate working hours.

guide	**show**

The professor guided/showed us through progressive steps to learn the lesson.

terminate	**lapse**

The semester terminated/lapsed after submitting our final papers.

Exercise 6-B

Revise these sentences to make them assuredly uncertain.

1. Physical chemistry is important for marital bliss.

2. Defensive driving is ineffective.

3. Over-eating causes human beings to become over weight.

4. Rain storms cause flooding.

5. Rest and drinking fluids are the best remedy to recover from the flu.

6. Swimming is the best exercise for working all parts of the human body.

7. Great novels are written by Russian authors.

8. Preschools assist children in becoming better overall students.

GENERALIZATIONS

Use the verb *tend* for qualifying or defending a generalization.

Examples: People *tend* to have less money to spend since the recession hit.

Chicago's winter weather *tends* to get windy and cold.

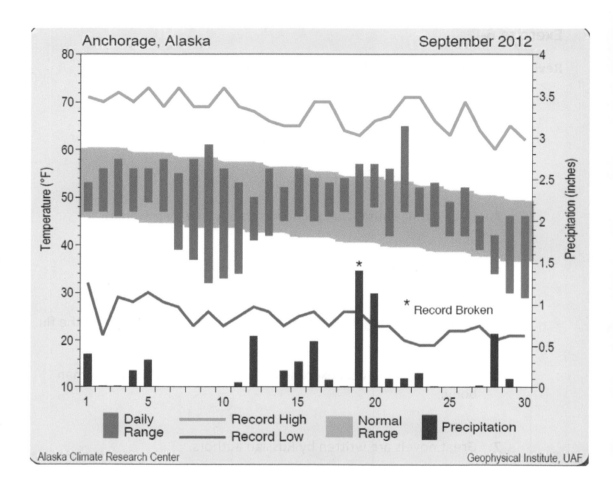

Alaska Climate Research Center, Geophysical Institute, UAF

Figure F-1

(Sample data commentary)

Figure 6-1 shows the temperatures and precipitation recorded in Anchorage, Alaska, during September of 2012. As can be seen, records illustrate high volatility. During September 19-20, temperatures leveled at colder records generating snow. At the same period of time, daily ranges broke weather records. This trend resulted in precipitation amounting to 1.5 inches.

VERBS FREQUENTLY USED IN DATA COMMENTS:

ACTIVE VERBS	*PASSIVE* FORM
contain	contained in
demonstrate	demonstrated in
depict	depicted in
display	displayed in
give	given in
illustrate	illustrated in
indicate	indicated in
list	listed in
present	presented in
provide	provided in
report	reported in
reveal	revealed in
show	shown in
suggest	suggested in
summarize	summarized in

Terminology for Graphs

These terms can be used to describe graphs' different points or areas.

Distinct point on graph

peak   The temperature peaked at midnight to 104 degrees Fahrenheit.
The *peak* of 104 degrees Fahrenheit was reached by midnight.
(The word peak may be used as a noun or verb.)

Distinct points

peak	high point	local/global maximum
low point		local/global minimum

Area on a graph

spike   There was an upward *spike* in the stock market during the
previous quarter.
The stock market *spiked* upward during the previous quarter.
(The word spike may be used as a noun or verb.)

Areas

Increase	upward trend	sharp rise			
decrease	downward trend	fall off	steep fall	decline	dip
level off	remain steady	little or no fluctuation			
spike (negative or positive)					

Time Phrases

In addition, be aware of the proper time words.

From 7 AM to 9 AM	In the morning/afternoon/evening.....
Throughout the day	At night......
Until 5 PM	During the work day...

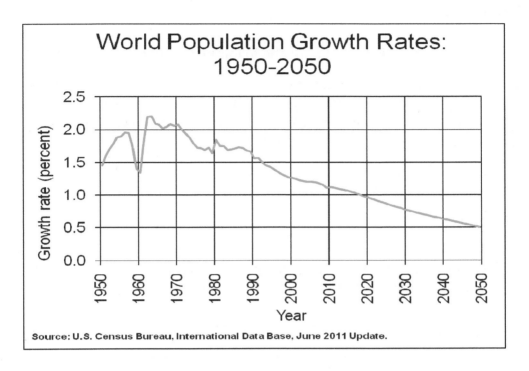

http://www.census.gov/population/international/data/idd/worldgraph.php

Figure F-2

In Figure F-2, World Population Growth Rates: 1950-2050, the growth rate rose from about 1.5 percent per year from 1950-51 to a peak of over 2 percent in the early 1960s due to reductions in mortality. Growth rates thereafter started to decline due to rising age at marriage, as well as increasing availability and use of effective contraceptive methods. Note that changes in population growth have not always been steady. A dip in the growth rate from1959-1960, for instance, was due to the Great Leap Forward in China. During that time, both natural disasters and decreased agricultural output in the wake of massive social reorganization caused China's death rate to rise sharply and its fertility rate to fall by almost half.

Exercise 6-C

Please look at graph F-2 and discuss the following questions.

1. What do you think about the visual representation of the bar graph F-2? Is anything missing? Would you include actual percentages? Would you include specific numbers? Would you add anything to the title? Would you add anything to the X or Y axes?

2. If you were writing a data commentary on this figure, what would you choose for your highlights? Please choose three.

    a. _____

    b. _____

    c. _____

3. What about the numbers? Are they self-explanatory?

4. Do you think anything in the line graph is misleading? Why or why not?

5. Any other comments/observations?

Problem Areas

As you delve into research, you most likely will encounter situations whereby your results are quite different than expected. Seize the moment to posit yourself as a well-informed researcher and discuss the problems as constructive criticism. An uncomplicated solution to resolve such future predicaments may indeed assist others in your field of study. This diversion may spark awareness in a parallel area of interest. You will be commended for your honesty and forthright style of discussion.

These suggested verb phrases may help in presenting your explanation.

…may be due to the fact…

…may have contributed to the shortcomings…

…could have negatively attributed to the…

…would have probably accounted for…

Samples:

This miscalculation may be due to the fact that…

Inconsistencies in gathering samples may have contributed to the shortcomings…

Inaccurate data could have negatively attributed to the…

Incomplete answers on the questionnaires would have probably accounted for…

```
Rank, Site, No. of Incident cases, Proportion

All sites 264,131 /100.0

1          Stomach              66,440 /25.2

2          Lung                 38,052 /14.4

3          Colon                30,201 /11.4

4          Liver                25,000 /9.5

5          Rectum               17,466 /6.6

6          Prostate             11,304 /4.3

7          Esophagus            9,992 /3.8

8          Pancreas             9,440 /3.6

9          Bladder              8,471 /3.2

10         Lymphoid tissue      7,769 /2.9

Others                          39,996 /15.1
```

Figure F-3

Number and Proportion of Cancer Incident Cases in Japan (Males, 1995)

Sample Data Commentary

Figure F-3 shows the number and proportion of cancer incident cases in Japanese males in 1995. As can be seen in the data, over one quarter accounted for stomach cancer. Moreover, about half of these cancers occurred in the digestive system: stomach, colon, esophagus, rectum, duodenum, and intestine. On the other hand, at that time, only 14% accounted for lung cancer. Overall, the figure suggests Japanese males tend to develop digestive cancer; especially, of the stomach, this may tend to have a relationship with their appetite tendency.

Exercise 6-D

1. In what term has the writer comparatively interpreted the numbers?

2. What definitive cancer evaluation has the author expressed towards the end of the paragraph?

3. What has the author concluded?

4. In the last sentence, name the three verbs used to show hedging.

Exercise 6-E

POPULAR CAR COLORS IN THE U.S.A. (GENDER SPECIFIC)		
Color	**Gender**	**Percentage**
Silver	women/men	24%
White	women	20%
Black	men	15%
Gray	men	14%
Green	women	10%
Blue	women/men	9%
Red	women/men	8%

Figure F-4

Write a short data commentary (5 sentences) using the information from Figure F-4. Remember to begin with a summary statement, add a linking *as-clause*, write two support sentences, and finish up with a concluding sentence.

_____

_____

_____

_____

_____

_____

_____

_____

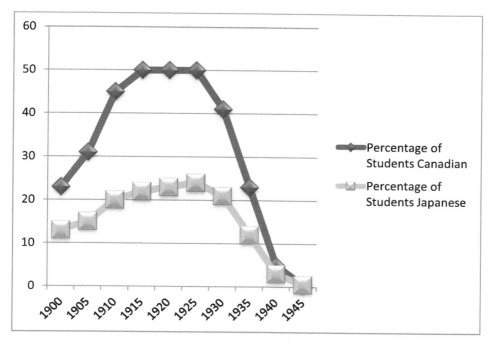

Figure F-5: Percentages of Canadian & Japanese Students in U.S. Colleges & Universities (at 5 year intervals)

CANADIAN STUDENTS = diamonds (black)

JAPANESE STUDENTS = squares (grey)

Practice Writing

Now, it is your turn to write a data commentary.

Type a data commentary by interpreting Figure F-5's information in your own words. (one paragraph, 5 sentences, double spaced, and a title)

Remember to use the appropriate vocabulary which follows when interpreting data commentaries:

curve   peak   spike   upward trend   sharp rise   increase

decrease   downward trend   fall off   steep fall   decline   dip

level off   remain steady   little or no fluctuation

spike (positive or negative)   low point   high point

(Also, use the verbs previously listed in this section.)

SECTION 7

Paraphrasing, Plagiarism & Summarizing

HOW TO PARAPHRASE

Paraphrasing is simply taking an original writing and transforming it into your own words without changing the meaning; always giving credit to the original author with citations. Rightfully so, you may reconstruct the original sentences into your own writing style, sentence structure, vocabulary choice, and word order; at the same time, flawlessly merging them into your own body of text. Meanwhile, these paraphrases naturally flow within your writing since all of the text was composed by you; thus, the motivation for paraphrasing. Although it is acceptable to use quotations in your papers, always be sure to use quotes sparingly since it tends to disrupt the writer's flow. Do not merely substitute synonyms when paraphrasing. For example:

original   *Business people ride the commuter train to work.*

incorrect   *Workers take the commuter train to work.*
paraphrase

better   *Commuters travel by train to work.*
paraphrase

As you can see, the incorrect paraphrase just changes *business people* to *workers* and *ride* to *take*. This is not a suitable paraphrase. The better paraphrase; first, condenses the sentence; changes the nouns (*business people*) to *commuters;* and changes the verb (*ride*) to (*travel*).

ORIGINAL SENTENCE: Any intelligent fool can make things bigger and more complex... It takes a touch of genius - and a lot of courage to move in the opposite direction. **Albert Einstein**

Is this paraphrase a reasonable representation of the original?

PARAPHRASE SENTENCE: The intellectual may be thought a fool when bravely progressing towards a reverse course, abstaining from creating extra intricate objects. **Albert Einstein**

This method of paraphrasing sentence by sentence using synonym substitution can often be successful, but you will most likely **not** demonstrate your full understanding of the passage. Another weakness is that the resulting summary is not original and would be considered plagiarism by many people. Simple synonym substitution is often not considered to be original work. Far more needs to be changed from the original source. **A better but more difficult strategy for summary writing would be to carefully consider what elements are important, put the original away, and write down what you have understood.** This may allow you to condense the ideas in the source even further.

When you write a formal summary of someone else's ideas, you should keep in mind the following guidelines. (Remember, if you are taking notes for yourself, direct copying is OK, but it is a good idea to indicate in your notes when you are directly copying.)

1. Always try to use your own words, except for technical key terms.

2. Include enough support and detail so that the presentation is clear.

3. Do not try to paraphrase specialized vocabulary or technical terms.

4. Include nothing more than what is contained in the original. (Do not include your own comments or evaluation.)

5. Make sure the summary reads smoothly. Use enough transitional devices and supporting detail. You do not want a collection of sentences that do not flow.

Why paraphrase?

Paraphrasing is using your own words to report someone else's material or ideas. A paraphrase allows you to use another writer's material to support a point you are making in your own work without using the other writer's exact wording. You will probably use paraphrasing when you want to change the style or the language used in the original, either to make it easier to understand or to make it fit better into your own piece of writing. Unlike a summary, a paraphrase is usually about the same length as the original, but both the words and the sentence structure of the original must be changed in the paraphrase. If you are paraphrasing a sentence, the length of the paraphrase can be the same, longer or shorter, and you should just reword the phrases without changing meaning. Focus on the *meaning* of the original sentence in your paraphrase.

Exercise 7-A

Look at the following statements and then the paraphrased versions. Write "A" for acceptable and "U" for unacceptable. If the paraphrase is unacceptable, rewrite it.

1. (original)   States with laws allowing drivers to drive higher than 65 mph have a higher occurrence of accidents; as well as, a higher mortality rate.

   (paraphrase) States shouldn't have speed limit laws.

   _____

2. (original)   The stock market frequently changes in reaction to international political events.

   (paraphrase) The global situation impacts the ups and downs of the stock market.

   _____

3. (original)   Technology can be an adversity at a company if there are no IT managers.

   (paraphrase) A business needs technology to be successful.

   _____

4. (original)   If there were any possibility of surviving a nuclear war, we would not have to disarm.

   (paraphrase) We need to stop making nuclear weapons since they could demolish everything.

   _____

5. (original)   The decline of the American family is one reason for youth violence in today's culture.

   (paraphrase) The problems young people have in America today can be linked to the disintegration of the family unit.

   _____

6. (original)   When making a cake, you first need to assemble and sift together the dry ingredients.

   (paraphrase) Put the flour and eggs together.

   _____

BETTER PARAPHRASING

Original

A smartphone is a device that lets you make telephone calls, but also adds in features that, in the past, you would have found only on a personal digital assistant or a computer--such as the ability to send and receive e-mail and edit office documents.

Choose the better paraphrase:

Paraphrase A

A type of cell phone is the smartphone that not only allows one to send and receive telephone calls, yet offers much more in the way of revising office text. Previously, separate devices (personal digital assistants {PDAs} or computers) could only achieve these tasks.

Paraphrase B

Recently, a very popular new mobile phone has hit the markets, the smartphone. How did we live without our smartphones before? Making phone calls is not the only feature, with all kinds of apps we can play games, take better photos, answer e-mails, and so much more. Forget about your outdated cell phones since smartphones are on the rise!

Which paraphrase is the better one? If you chose A over B, you are correct. In order to paraphrase well, search out new vocabulary words which express the original meaning without distortion. Thus, changing the words, not the meaning. Paraphrase B incorrectly changes the original meaning by adding additional information ("Recently, a very popular new mobile, with all kinds of apps we can play games, take better photos, has hit the markets" implies that it was just introduced to the public; making assumptions that we previously experienced hard times and condemning regular cell phones). Also, important details are deleted (PDAs, computers, and edit office documents).

Exercise 7-B

Paraphrasing

Remember, a good paraphrase delivers the same meaning of the original context with different words and word order. A bad paraphrase distorts the original meaning and may even delete or add information that was never in the original.

Choose the better paraphrase.

1.

Original: Disco dancing was all the rage during the 1970s. Young people would flock to the popular disco clubs to dance the Hustle, bus stop, and bump, just to name a few. A whole new genre of music sprang out of this movement.

Paraphrase A: In the 1970s, disco dancing was very popular. So much so, that disco clubs were full of everyone dancing to their favorite songs as they Hustled, bus stopped and bumped their ways around the dance floor.

Paraphrase B: The 1970s witnessed disco dancing which quite often led to contests for the best dancer. Everyone would enjoy dancing to the DJ's pick of songs until the evening culminated with the contest. The winner would smile all the way to the bank with his (or her) winnings!

2.

Original: Successfully completing a college degree in a timely manner can be challenging these days. Often, summers are filled with mandatory courses not fulfilled during fall and spring semesters. Another option students may be forced to resort to are evening classes to help ease the load. All in all, be flexible in scheduling classes.

Paraphrase A: Finishing college degrees can be difficult at times. Most students do not want to attend school at night or ruin their summers. Relax and take your time if your parents are paying the bill. Enjoying this time of your life before resorting to working a job.

Paraphrase B: When college students need to finish their degrees as efficiently as possible, there are three ways to achieve this. Look for summer school, evening, and online courses that will help accomplish this goal when enrolling in classes.

3.

Original: Living on your own may seem the best way to gain independence. Yet, many responsibilities are necessary for success. Just to name a few, money budgeting, cooking, and laundry play a major role in everyday life. Your own level of maturity will contribute positively to such a way of life.

Paraphrase A: Life is good living on your own! No one is there telling you what to do. All of these responsibilities are working out great since there is plenty of money for take-out every night, and my girlfriend does all my laundry. The only drawback is my job is temporary for the summer!

Paraphrase B: In order to achieve an independent lifestyle, a high level of maturity must be attained. Conscientious daily tasks are extremely important when considering budget, meals, and clothing.

Disassembling Sentences into Acceptable Paraphrases

When asked to paraphrase an original written text, focus on the following:

1. First and foremost, attempt to comprehend the writing in its entirety after reading the text as many times as deemed necessary.

2. Discern what to highlight and begin summarizing these topics in your own words.

3. *Shared language* is the specific vocabulary used as technical terminology within your own discipline of study. By using this type of language, you are not plagiarizing. Therefore, do not change nor quote shared language.

4. Your goal should entail not using any major original words; except for, proper nouns (names/locations) and technical terms. If and when you cannot avoid this, use quotation marks around the words and/or phrases. Try to quote as little as possible.

5. It is fine to use quotations from the original in your paraphrase. Just remember to give credit where credit is due.

6. Paraphrases must <u>always</u> be cited with parentheses on the same page and a reference page entry. Remember, the original idea you have paraphrased still belongs to the original author; therefore, give credit through citations.

7. When to paraphrase: at times, when you can type something in simpler terms and when using facts.

8. Use extreme caution in keeping track of your source information as not to mistakenly plagiarize.

Take a look at the following sample paragraph:

Have you ever noticed how tourists mob the cable cars in San Francisco? When the workforce of this city embarks on their way to work, they also use the famed cars as transit. Just as visitors to this metropolis enjoy riding to the well-known Fisherman's Wharf and Ghiradelli Square, at the same time, stylishly dressed business people and students ride the rails to their destinations. This public conveyance has been serving San Francisco since the late 1800s and will continue for many years to come.

Vocabulary:

cable car – noun - a vehicle, usually enclosed, used on a cable railway or tramway

mob – verb – crowd

embark – verb – to board a vehicle

metropolis – noun - city

rails – noun - tracks

conveyance – noun – transportation

Sentence Structure Modifications

The first step in paraphrasing is changing the structure of the original sentence. One may focus on beginning your paraphrase at a different spot in the paragraph. In the process, undoubtedly, changes in phrasing will be necessary. Additionally, you will reduce wordiness, replace words and phrases, and eliminate prepositional phrases with possessive forms. For example, a few different places to begin paraphrasing may be: "When the city's workforce…," "Just as visitors …," "…stylishly dressed business …," or "This public conveyance…"

- *When the city's workforce…* Possible paraphrase of first sentence: The city's workforces alongside tourists mob the famed San Francisco cable cars.
- *Just as visitors…* Possible paraphrase of body text: Sightseers like riding these cars to the renowned Fisherman's Wharf and Ghiradelli Square.
- *…stylishly dressed business …* Possible paraphrase of body text: Additionally, smartly clothed workers and students join this rush hour journey.
- *This public conveyance…* Possible paraphrase of body text: Close to the turn of the 20th century, these cable cars served the public well and will carry on in the foreseeable future.

Another method would be to begin with different nouns. Such as, "Fisherman's Wharf," "Ghirardelli Square," "San Francisco," San Franciscans," "Business people," or "Students." Here, the focus is shifted to a range of other nouns, while still maintaining the original ideas.

- *Fisherman's Wharf and Ghirardelli Square are popular destinations for sightseers traveling on busy cable cars.*
- *San Francisco has preserved historic cable cars, as a result, city dwellers commute on this public transportation system during rush hour.*
- *San Franciscans enjoy the cable cars as a means to commute.*
- *Business people ride the rails to their jobs.*
- *Students board the cable cars on their way to school.*

Synonym Replacement

Keeping in mind that you do not want to change the meaning, you may replace words or phrases with synonyms. While altering some of these words, you may find that your structure needs to be changed once again, and that is just fine.

Final Paraphrase

San Francisco has preserved historic cable cars, as a result, city dwellers commute on this public transportation system during rush hour. Additionally, Fisherman's Wharf and Ghirardelli Square are popular destinations for sightseers traveling on busy cable cars. San Franciscans enjoy the cable cars as a means to commute. While business people ride the rails to their jobs, students board the cable cars on their way to school.

Do you think this is a suitable paraphrase?

Exercise 7-C

Paraphrase Writing

Paraphrase the following paragraph:

During the twentieth century, diners became a part of American culture as travelers sought out places to eat while driving throughout the diverse states of America. These diners were manufactured in a few standardized sizes and shapes modeled after railroad dining cars. Convenience in grabbing a quick good meal on the road was the intent of these eateries. Owners of such diners outfitted them with distinctive décor native to that part of the country. Menus boasted of their local products and quite often gained a reputation for tasty dishes, as regular customers steadfastly returned to these establishments. The diners' waiters and waitresses were noted for their friendliness, outspoken approach, spirited energy and at times, their outlandish behavior. Although many of these diners have not survived over the years, those still intact are relished.

Vocabulary:

diner – noun - restaurant built to resemble a dining train car (or in some cases an actual converted dining car) from 1935 and on.

diverse – adjective – varied, different

outfitted – verb – equipped

distinctive – adjective – unique

boasted – verb – bragged, showed off

steadfastly - adverb – loyally

outlandish – adjective - bizarre, eccentric

intact – adjective – unharmed

relish – verb – enjoy, delight in

Enter your paraphrase below:

_____

_____

_____

_____

_____

_____

_____

Quoting, Paraphrasing, & Summarizing (The Differences)

Quoting is taking the same exact words from an author and using them in your writing. Always cite the author and source.

Paraphrasing is transforming an author's original words into your own words. This material is generally shorter in length and more concise than the original. Always cite the author and source.

Summarizing is writing about the main idea and its main points in your own words. This material is quite shorter as an overview of the original. Always cite the author and source.

These three ways of blending other authors' works into your own writings are very different. Therefore, when planning your papers, allow for a variance of these techniques if they enhance your material. Quotations, paraphrasing, and summarizing may be utilized to:

- give meaningful background.

- supply support and reliability.

- offer differing points of view.

- contribute samples of previous work related to your own.

- emphasize a point that you either have the same opinion or differ.

- stress a significant writing.

- detach (or distance) yourself from an original, clearly as an opponent.

WRITING SUMMARIES

When asked to summarize a published writing, follow consistent steps to accomplish this task.

1. Skim (quickly read over) the text, making note of the different sections, bold headings, subheadings, and graphics.

2. Reread - for meaning. Do not stop to look up vocabulary; just try to comprehend the general meaning and tone of the writing.

3. 3rd reading - more specific. Highlight each section's main ideas, support facts, areas that merit review, and the author's purposes for presenting this perspective. Do not summarize areas that seem too detailed or nonessential. Now, you have an outline of each section you will summarize.

4. In your own words, write the main idea for each section in good quality sentence form. Continue with support, clarifying key points, and omit needless details.

5. Write your thesis statement. By reviewing your main idea sentences, you can construct your thesis statement which clearly states the main points of the writing. (See next lesson for specifics on writing thesis statements.)

6. Now, you may begin to assemble your summary. Begin your first paragraph with the title and author of the piece being summarized. You may weave your thesis statement into your first sentence. Otherwise, you may choose to begin with a hook to get the reader's attention, followed by background information; ending your first paragraph with a thesis statement.

7. Each new paragraph presents the author's main ideas with support information as the body, written in your own words. It's usually best to adhere to the same order of information that the text originally followed. Do not forget to insert transitions to contribute to nice flow throughout your summary. Follow the checklist below when constructing your paper.

   a. Be sure to cite the title and author of the original writing.

   b. Write in the present tense.

   c. Be concise and much briefer than the original text. Remember, this is a summary which is a short review.

   d. If using any of the author's original words, cite those using accepted English methods.

   e. This is not a platform for your own comments and observations. A summary simply gives an overview review of a given text, remaining true to the author.

8. Proofread your writing by reading it aloud to yourself. Of upmost importance is that you clearly communicate the author's main ideas without distorting the original meaning. Make sure that everything is flowing, so that your reader is nicely guided throughout the summary. Make sure that you have honestly expressed yourself here in your own words, not the original author's. Bear in mind that you may always cite a direct quote from the author, but the summary assignment is largely expected to be in your own words.

9. Revise for spelling, punctuation, and grammar. It may be a good idea to have a native English speaker read the summary. Some areas may need attention for clear comprehension.

Creating Your Thesis Statement

What is a Thesis Statement?

A thesis statement is a specific writing plan that states an opinion, not facts. It furnishes the main idea with specific, not general support that previews exactly what points you will cover in your paper. It is located in the first paragraph and serves as the initial guiding point at the start of your text. It may be one or two sentences. Do not try to prepare this important element of your paper at the onset of writing. After much reading and research, begin to assemble evidence; explore specific connections as contrasts and/or similarities; and consider the importance of these connections as related to your topic. From that point, you will have a significant amount of knowledge to formulate a preliminary thesis statement; later, fine-tune it while further work ensues in composing your paper.

Most often, a thesis statement is positioned as the last sentence in your introductory paragraph. Therefore, your first sentence begins with a hook to get your reader's attention. Then, this paragraph progresses to giving background information in the next sentence or two. Finally, your last sentence or two present a clear thesis statement with the main idea and support. This must be clearly stated so your reader has complete understanding of what is being addressed here. Also, you may begin your introductory paragraph with the thesis statement, continuing with background information, and ending with a hook.

Quite frequently, papers written at the higher education level are based on persuasion. Professors assign research and subsequent writing assignments that take the form of academic arguments. Begin with a brief introduction and background of your topic; then, proceed with a sentence or two stating your point of view (opinion). Believe it or not, you have just written your thesis statement as your opinion.

Illustration

Perhaps you must write on the advantages and disadvantages of marriage in this day and age, for a course you are taking. Remember, your thesis statement must be an opinion that may be challenged. Take a look at this developing thesis statement.

Married people are faithful to their lifestyles for various reasons.

This thesis statement is weak since it simply states general information, neither specific nor opinionated. Think deeper about the pros and cons of being married, plus some specific reasons that may portray this lifestyle.

While married people view their lifestyle as dependent, many couples may argue that their union leads to independence.

As you can see, this edited thesis statement supplies two differing opinions that will eventually spawn a debate with more specific viewpoints on dependency and independency within marriage. Thus, you have a developing thesis statement that may well take another form as you delve further into researching your topic. Of course, this thesis statement may be revised as you see fit.

Do I really need a thesis statement?

If you are perplexed whether your paper requires a thesis statement, follow these general guidelines.

1. Ask the instructor.

2. In all probability, you must create a thesis statement and persuasively defend it if assignments require any of the following:

    - compare and contrast

    - analyzing

    - interpretation

    - cause and effect

    - defending an issue

Thesis Statement Rules

A thesis statement should:

- be limited to mentioning only those points you plan to discuss in your writing.

- never be so broad that it's difficult to discuss all relevant information.

- do not present various ideas.

- not contain two conflicting ideas.

EXAMPLES

1. (Three experiences) [2] make a (trip to Hawaii) [1] a magnificent vacation.

2. (The western world is adapting to eastern medicinal practices) [1] for (specific natural therapies). [2]

3. (Pets)[1] can be a (source of comfort, joy, and companionship to human beings).[2]

4. (People are living longer these days and attribute their good health)[1] to (a few daily practices).[2]

main idea, topic[1]   support[2]

Exercise 7-D

Name the problems affecting these thesis statements.

PROBLEMS
a. conflicting ideas   b. open-ended question   c. too broad   d. not limited

1. The Illinois State Fair in Springfield was a disaster because of the way the press criticized the way it was run, but it was exciting for little children and had many good food booths. _____

2. Television commercials are obnoxious to the person who is intent on watching a good show; on the other hand, they provide entertainment in the behavior of the performers and they provide a good chance to take a snack break. _____

3. Since politicians are constantly bombarding each other, how do they expect anyone to know who is right and who is wrong? _____

4. Rap music is a popular form of art because it is creative and unique and because it follows the traditions of other unexpectedly developed music like jazz. _____

5. Unless people are mindful of pollution, the earth will be damaged by the year 2050. _____

How to write a thesis statement - To create a thesis statement simply follow this formula:

YOUR TOPIC   +   YOUR OPINION   =   THESIS STATEMENT

<u>**Your topic (subject)**</u>   **+**   <u>**your opinion**</u>   **=**   <u>**thesis statement**</u>

vegetarians   +   are healthier   =

Thesis statement: *It seems that vegetarians are healthier than meat eaters.*

fit people   +   live longer   =

Thesis statement: *Fit people live longer and healthier lives.*

USING HOOKS WITHIN AN INTRODUCTORY PARAGRAPH

The first paragraph presents an introduction on the topic. Your opening sentence/sentences can attract your audience by supplying a hook. A first-class hook will make your readers want to continue reading.

1. Beginning with a question is a popular method; wherein, your readers will be eager to learn the answer, be hooked, and enticed to read.

    How can our earth support population growth at such an astounding rapid rate of increase?

    The majority of readers will not know the answer, most likely be hooked by nature of curiosity, and continue reading for the answer.

2. The second approach may be to write an observation hook to draw interest from the readers.

    These days, people are digging deeper in their pockets to buy a cup of coffee in Italy.

    This statement spurs reader interest to discover what is going on in Italy.

3. The third approach presents a situation that hooks the
    audience to discover what is happening.

    *Traveling through this space as a weightless form invokes
    feelings of freedom and hushed calm. Its span of graceful
    beauty supports life forms unique to the habitat.*

    Hooked yet? Does this scenario persuade you to continue
    reading? This hook describes scuba divers' ventures down
    deep.

4. At times, writers employ a direct quote.

    *"Four score and seven years ago our fathers brought forth on this
    continent, a new nation, conceived in Liberty, and dedicated to the
    proposition that all men are created equal." 1863*

    Abraham Lincoln's Gettysburg Address begins as a hook on the
    topic of equality.

As you can see, there are various ways to begin writing and garner your
audience's attention. By all means, **do not** begin writing in simplistic terms. For
example:

*   This paper's main topic is evolution.
*   I am going to write about the evolution of mankind.

Readers will not be convinced to continue reading.

Introductory Paragraph with Hook, Background & Thesis Statement

Cheaper power can demolish the world! [1] *Oil has sustained our technology for many years at a lower efficiency rate. Recently, green energy sources have emerged, but they are costly and impractical.* [2] *Herein, negative points concerning nuclear weapons, global warming, and nuclear accidents will be discussed.* [3]

[1]   hook
[2]   background information
[3]   thesis statement with 3 main points (nuclear weapons, global warming & nuclear accidents)

Exercise 7-E

Read the sentence below and write 3-5 main points that will be stated in a thesis statement. (Name some of the nuclear power energy advantages.)

The advantages of nuclear power include several earth friendly benefits.

1.   _____

2.   _____

3.   _____

4.   _____

5.   _____

Now, use only 3 of those points to prepare for your thesis statement which states an opinion.

For example: more efficient, decreases the need of foreign biofuels, no carbon dioxide, pollutes the air

Thesis statement: _____

_____

SUMMARIES CONTINUED

After you have successfully created a good hook in your introductory paragraph, your next statements will give background (or historical) information on your main topic. Finishing up the paragraph with a thesis statement will present the plan guiding your reader into your summary.

Body Paragraphs

Each body paragraph begins with a **clear topic sentence** which supports your thesis statement. The body of your paper points out new points related to the main idea. Continue to refer back to your thesis statement on a regular basis, so you do not stray from the main focus of the paper. Strive to write a clear first statement that will foretell what the paragraph is concerning. Don't forget to utilize transitional words and phrases to guide your readers through the text. Also, development should include vital tactics to convince readers of your cause. Utilize graphics and models, refer to data, analyze texts, link in related stories, you may need to define some terms, compare, contrast, and evaluate. **Well-constructed supporting details** then continue to clarify the main idea of the topic sentence. Meaningful, accurate, and uncomplicated elements are written to transmit your point in the clearest communication as possible. In order to guide your reader, repeat key words or synonyms of them. The **organization** of your paragraph is fundamental to conveying consistency beginning with a succinct topic sentence; subsequently, expanding upon additional supportive details. The order of such details should maintain the same order as they were presented in the topic sentence. Attention to **cohesiveness** will allow all of your sentences to flow together as a whole. Your ultimate goal is to create a text that easily joins ideas in a sensible manner; guiding your reader from one thought to the next. This is a learned technique achieved by persistent analysis of writing samples and practicing your hand at this craft.

EXAMPLE: Paper Title   **How to Assimilate into American Culture**

INTRODUCTORY PARAGRAPH

Hook: Absorb yourself into English and the American way of life in no time! Countless hours of studying English by memorizing vocabulary, dialogues, conjugating verbs, grammar drills, and conversation mixers can subject a student to burnout. There must be an easier way to learn a language. Assimilation into American culture requires complete daily immersion, an outgoing attitude, and fearless optimism.

FIRST BODY PARAGRAPH

Undeniably, leaving comfort zones to take in a new culture every day can prove to be very rewarding. To begin with, living from morning to night in an American English speaking environment is a win-win situation. As Americans, we welcome international visitors and would like to assist in any possible way. For most students, this is a once in a lifetime experience and taking full advantage of such a short-lived opportunity makes complete sense. Steadily, your global view will expand; new opportunities will be obtainable as new horizons materialize for your future.

SAMPLE INITIAL PHRASES

Herewith, are several phrases that may help you get started in writing better English academic papers. There are six sections giving sample phrases in the following categories:

1. Introductions
2. Reviews
3. Explanations with investigation
4. Definitions
5. Debate
6. Conclusions

Introductions

The following research begins by clarifying...

This investigation concerns several...

Sections A and B focus on ...

The next chapter begins...

In order to introduce the research topic...

Reviews

This study makes a strong case for...

This study neglects to take into account ...

This work has proven to be stellar in...

Several novel and significant approaches have been...

In reviewing the material, there is little support...

The research offers a simple analysis of...

Explanations with investigation

There is little evidence to support that...

Substantial evidence in this study suggests that...

One may propose that...

The relevance of this work is inconsequential since...

In final analysis, it is crucial not to overlook...

Ever present, is the critical distinction between...

Definitions

Current understanding of _____ may be unclear; yet, …

Fundamental to this study is…

This research was intentionally designed to investigate the hypothesis that…

Earlier studies have advocated that…

The main focus of this paper is…

The basic query to scrutinize in this article is…

Debate

The point taken here is principally appropriate to…

To rephrase this point in another way…

A significant drawback of this theory is…

This brings up for discussion whether…

The point is well taken, but…

This strengthens the argument that…

Conclusions

Drawing to a close, this study's results…

In the final analysis, quite a few questions have surfaced for future studies.

Finally, proposal suggestions for reform will be considered.

As implied in this assessment, our future holds the answers to many questions discussed here.

As addressed in this article, many key issues still need…

While the findings here are quite impressive, further research is necessary to…

PLAGIARISM

Plagiarism is taking credit for someone else's ideas or published words, (paper form and/or the Internet) where credit is not due. As one pursues knowledge in given areas of concentration, one is engaged in numerous reading assignments, lectures, and discussions full of noted authorities words of wisdom. In the United States, plagiarism is considered very serious. Therefore, do not take this matter lightly. When assigned specific writing assignments requiring assimilation of noted author's ideas, please be sure to paraphrase the information. Simply read the author's text several times (section by section), put it away, and write in paraphrase form (your own words) what you have just read and absorbed. Do not look at the original writing while paraphrasing to encourage composing thoughtful original text on your own.

In order to avoid plagiarism, give credit when you make use of

> ➢ another's idea, hypothesis, or viewpoint.

> ➢ graphs, tables, statistics, drawings, facts (that are not common knowledge).

> ➢ another's quotations.

Recognizing plagiarism

Compare this original text with the paraphrased versions.

> **Papiamento** (or **Papiamentu**) is the most widely spoken language on the Caribbean ABC islands, having official status on the islands of

Aruba and Curaçao. The language is also recognized on Bonaire by the Dutch government. Papiamento is a Creole language derived from African languages and either Portuguese or Spanish, with some influences from Amerindian languages, English, and Dutch. Papiamento has two main dialects: *Papiamento*, spoken primarily on Aruba; and *Papiamentu*, spoken primarily on Bonaire and Curaçao. There are various local development theories. One such theory proposes that Papiamento developed in the Caribbean from an original Portuguese-African pidgin used for communication between African slaves and Portuguese slave traders, with later Dutch and Spanish (and even some Aruac Indian) influences. The Judaeo-Portuguese population of the ABC islands increased substantially after 1654, when the Portuguese recovered the Dutch-held territories in Northeast Brazil – causing most of the Portuguese-speaking Jews in those lands to flee from religious persecution. The precise role of Sephardic Jews in the early development is unclear, but it is certain that Jews play a prominent role in the later development of Papiamento. Many early residents of Curaçao were Sephardic Jews either from Portugal, Spain, or Portuguese Brazil. Therefore, it can be assumed that Judaeo-Spanish was brought to the island of Curaçao, where it gradually spread to other parts of the community. As the Jewish community became the prime merchants and traders in the area, business and everyday trading was conducted in Papiamento with some Ladino influences. While various nations owned the island and official

languages changed with ownership, Papiamento became the
constant language of the residents.

http://en.wikipedia.org/wiki/Papiamento

Unacceptable, plagiarized version

Papiamento (or **Papiamentu**) is the most used spoken language on
the Caribbean ABC islands (Aruba, Curacao & Bonaire), having
official status on the islands of Aruba and Curaçao. It is also
recognized on Bonaire by the Dutch government. Papiamento is a
Creole language taken from African languages and either
Portuguese or Spanish, with some influences from Amerindian
languages, English, and Dutch. Papiamento has two main dialects:
Papiamento, spoken mostly on Aruba; and *Papiamentu*, spoken
mostly on Bonaire and Curaçao. One such theory proposes that
Papiamento developed in the Caribbean from an original
Portuguese-African pidgin used for communication between African
slaves and Portuguese slave traders, with later Dutch and Spanish
(and even some Aruac Indian) influences. The Judaeo-Portuguese
population of the ABC islands grew substantially after 1654, when
the Portuguese recovered the Dutch-held territories in Northeast
Brazil – causing most of the Portuguese-speaking Jews in those
lands to leave from religious persecution. The precise role of
Sephardic Jews in the early development is unclear. Many early
residents of Curaçao were Sephardic Jews either from Portugal,
Spain, or Portuguese Brazil. Therefore, it can be assumed that

Judaeo-Spanish was brought to the island of Curaçao, where it gradually spread to other parts of the community. As the Jewish community became the prime merchants and traders in the area, business and everyday trading was conducted in Papiamento with some Ladino influences. While various nations owned the island and official languages changed with ownership, Papiamento stood firm as the language of the residents.

➤ The writer here has simply changed around some of the words, phrases, and order of the words. At times, the original words have been substituted with synonyms.

➤ The writer has not cited the original text or author for any of the original information.

Do not follow the example above, or you will be guilty of plagiarism. Additionally, by changing around some of the original wording, you run the risk or transforming the true intent of the original. By all means, do not change meaning when paraphrasing to avoid plagiarism.

Acceptable version

Papiamento (Papiamentu) is a language spoken on the Caribbean islands of Aruba, Bonaire, and Curacao where the islands' governments recognize the language. The dialect of Papiamento is spoken in Aruba, while the dialect of Papiamentu is spoken in Bonaire and Curacao. The origins of this language are believed to have been influenced by African languages, Portuguese, Spanish, English, Dutch and Amerindian languages. There are conflicting theories as to how the language developed. Some believe Papiamento grew out of an original Portuguese-African pidgin language, and later was influenced by Dutch and Spanish sea faring traders. After 1654, the Judaeo-Portuguese people of these islands grew significantly. The Jewish people greatly influenced this language in becoming merchants and traders in this Caribbean area. Papiamento was used in everyday language of business and bartering with Ladino influences. Today when traveling through the islands, one can distinctly hear Papiamento, and if you listen carefully and understand Spanish, you may understand the language for yourself.

http://en.wikipedia.org/wiki/Papiamento

> ➤ Do you think the writer has appropriately paraphrased from the original text?

> ➤ Is the original information accurately depicted without changing the meaning?

> ➤ If you could change this version, how would you rephrase it?

STRATEGIES FOR AVOIDING PLAGIARISM

- **Quote** everything coming directly from text, particularly while taking notes.

- **Paraphrase**, not just simply by rearranging or replacing a few words. Instead, read over what you want to paraphrase carefully; put it away, and write in paraphrase form (your own words) what you have just read and absorbed. Do not look at the original writing while paraphrasing to encourage composing thoughtful original text on your own. Now, write the author's ideas in your words.

- **Check your paraphrase** with the original text to make sure that you have not accidently used alike words and/or phrases. Check for accuracy of your written information, mindful of not altering the original meaning.

Generally speaking, common knowledge facts do not need to be quoted.

Common knowledge consists of facts found in abundant places and most likely are known by many people.

For example: *George Washington was the first president of the United States of America.* There is no need to quote this fact since this is information that many people know as common knowledge.

Nonetheless, facts that are not commonly known and novel ideas describing facts do need to be quoted.

For example: *"Early to bed, early to rise makes a man healthy, wealthy and wise."* Benjamin Franklin

"A bird in the hand is worth two in the bush." Greek storyteller Aesop

When quoting someone else's words, place quotation marks at the beginning and end of the phrase. Be sure that your ending punctuation is positioned inside the quotation marks. The source from which you have extracted the quote from must be documented. Become familiar with which particular standard documentation style your discipline uses.

Follow the rules for citing and follow them exactly. The following list cites some major standard documentation styles.

- Chicago Manual Style (CMS)
- Modern Language Association (MLA)
- American Psychological Association (APA)
- Oxford
- Harvard
- American Sociological Association (ASA)
- Vancouver
- other citation systems*

Paraphrasing: Most likely, this is the format you will use to integrate other sources into your original words. Even though your own words are paraphrasing here, do not forget to acknowledge the source of the information you have used.

*Go to the Word tool bar, references, and click on *Style.* A drop-down menu will appear with the major standard documentation styles; choose one, insert citation, and follow the directions. This software will format all of your input keystrokes for you.

Summaries: Writing a good summary requires accurate reading and the ability to find the main idea and most of the important supporting evidence in a piece of writing. Summaries are always quite a bit shorter than the original text, at times 75% shorter. Sometimes, particularly for a book, the summary is much shorter than the original. When you write a summary you give your readers an idea of the content of an article or book and save them the time and trouble of having to read the entire original. To write a good summary, keep in mind the following points:

1. Read the original carefully.

2. Mention the source and author at the beginning of the summary.

3. Mention the author's main idea without distorting those ideas or adding your own.

4. State the author's most important supporting evidence or sub points without distorting them. Do not include details.

5. Use your own wording. Occasionally, however, a phrase from the original may be especially striking, interesting or controversial. In that case you may use the authors' exact words if you put quotation marks around them.

6. Don't include your own ideas or comments. The summary should include only the author's ideas.

7. Periodically remind the reader that you are summarizing someone else's ideas.

Exercise 7-F

Read the following essay and complete the steps which follow, from:

Zenner, A. (2013), *Precise American Writing: A Guide for International Students and Professionals*, Marsten Publishing Group, Naperville, Illinois, USA

_____ (sub-heading)

All work and no play make for a dull life. This common expression may ring true for some Americans who are spending more and more time at work. Since World War II, Americans have added more hours to their daily work

schedule than ever before. At the present time, USA workers surpass every other industrialized country besides Japan in weekly hours worked.

_____ (sub-heading)

Although the standard work week hours remain at 40, a considerable amount of employees are working more weeks each year. At the same time, sick leave and paid time off for holidays have declined. Additionally, employees on monthly and/or weekly salaries, find themselves coming in earlier in the morning and staying much later at night. When given a job to do, they must fulfill these responsibilities no matter what time of day must be sacrificed.

_____ (sub-heading)

Stiff competition and sluggish productivity make for corporations pushing their employees to work longer hours. Many layoffs resulted in fewer people to do the same job while cutting costs. Lower paying jobs have forced these people to take on overtime and second jobs. Millions of Americans are surviving on two jobs each to just get by.

_____ (sub-heading)

Trading income for time could be one effective tactic for relieving the American worker. This is a cost free tactic; whereby, instead of offering yearly raises, companies could offer employees more free vacation time. These assured retreats are most likely to improve worker's performance and cut down on fatigue.

1. Label each paragraph above with a subheading indicating the subject discussed in that paragraph.

2. Which paragraph seems to state the main point of the article?

3. Write the main point here. _____

    _____

Practice Writing

Now, it is your turn to write a short one paragraph summary of this essay.

Remember to write in the present tense and begin your summary with a sentence that contains the source title, author, and the main idea. Use your own words, except for technical terms. Summarize the material in a balanced, neutral, and condensed approach. The summary should read smoothly using transitions and supporting detail.

YOUR NOTES

SECTION 8

Abstracts

ABSTRACTS

How will learning to write abstracts benefit me?

- ➤ ability to write detailed text in a succinctly communicative style
- ➤ ability to read abstracts more efficiently
- ➤ ability to better conduct research
- ➤ ability to develop new future abstracts
- ➤ ability to report data in a concise layout for database searches

An abstract is an abbreviated overview in paragraph form of a longer text. This original writing contains key words from the extended version. Subsequently, readers often use abstracts to recall these key points which are remindful of which source maintains particular conclusions. Compose your abstract in the same language as the research paper; interpreting it to one of the world languages, also. Since bibliographic references are included in informative abstracts, this is useful for readers writing up their own research and citing sources. By including exact search phrases and keywords (also referred to as search terms) to your abstracts, readers will be able to scan and find result listings. Perhaps overlooked in the past, cross-referencing through abstracts may possibly bring one to newer research areas.

Along with submitting an abstract and article for review, the author must also include a brief biography highlighting her/his academic achievements. In addition, the journal editors will offer "Guidelines for Authors" as to the particular format required. There are two types of abstracts: descriptive and informative. When asked to pen a descriptive abstract (also referred to as indicative), briefly describe in one paragraph the main topics listed in the table of contents. Readers will not expect a summarization of the facts or conclusions. This may not be the best approach in previewing such important work. For that reason, one may choose to write an informative abstract (at times, referred to as a structured abstract) concisely highlighting the article's main objectives in factual language, methods, results, and conclusions (it's unnecessary to include specific citations within the abstract). Characteristically, each section of your paper is represented by one single sentence in your abstract.

Finally, the process of writing an abstract is easiest to prepare after completing your research paper. Only then, will you be able to discern which text is best summarized as the important topics.

THE FOUR PARTS OF AN *INFORMATIVE* ABSTRACT

- Introduction/Objective (State objective, may include background information.)

- Methods (Briefly explain the procedure utilized to validate the research.)

- Results (Share highlighted observations plus/or data gathered.)

- Conclusion (Concisely assess the results. Confirm or negate hypothesis.)

Sample Informative Abstract

Journal of Rehabilitation Research and Development (Veteran's Administration)
Vol. 39 No. 1, January/February 2002
Pages 95 - 103

Personal Characteristics that Influence Exercise Behavior of Older Adults

Lisa W. Boyette, MEd; Adrienne Lloyd, MEd; James E. Boyette, MSICS; Erica Watkins, BA; Lori Furbush, PhD; Sandra B. Dunbar, PhD; L. Jerome Brandon, PhD

Atlanta VA Medical Center, Rehabilitation Research & Development Center, Atlanta, GA; Division of Geriatric Medicine and Gerontology, Emory University School of Medicine, Emory University, Atlanta, GA; Veterans Affairs, Health Eligibility Center, Atlanta, GA; Nell Hodgson Woodruff School of Nursing, Emory University School of Nursing, Emory University, Atlanta, GA; Department of Kinesiology and Health, Georgia State University, Atlanta, GA

Abstract: Long-term exercise participation among older adults will result in healthier lifestyles and reduced need for health care. A better understanding, therefore, of what influences older individuals to start and maintain exercise plans would be beneficial. The twofold purpose of this study was (1) to create a knowledge base of determinants that influence exercise behavior in older adults and (2) to have health professionals prioritize determinants that affect exercise initiation and adherence in older adults. The expert panel examined nine determinants within the category of personal characteristics: age, gender, ethnicity, occupation, educational level, socioeconomic status, biomedical status, smoking status, and past exercise participation. The experts rated the determinants on importance for influencing exercise behavior of older adults. This expert panel concluded that older adults who are in good health and have a history of exercise activity might be more likely to participate in long-term exercise programs.

Key words: aging; determinants; exercise.

http://www.rehab.research.va.gov/jour/02/39/1/absBoyette.htm

Sample Informative Abstract

International Journal of Behavioral Development, 32, 2008, pp. 290-297

Psychological Reactions to Israeli Occupation: Findings from the National Study of School-Based Screening in Palestine

Abdeen, Z., Qasrawi, R., Nabil, S., & Shaheen, M.

Children exposed to violent war-like and repeated political violence often experience a continued threat to life and their sense of safety, as well as a disruption of daily functioning. The purpose of the study was to examine the psychological impact of exposure to Israeli occupation on Palestinian school children in the West Bank and Gaza, Palestine. We assessed the association between exposure to occupation and the severity of posttraumatic symptoms and the inter-relationship between posttraumatic symptoms, functional impairment, somatic complaints, and coping strategies in school children. Palestinian students (n = 2100) from grades 9-11 were screened from both the West Bank (n = 1235) and Gaza (n = 724) and responded to self-report questionnaires. Results showed that extensive exposure to violence was associated with higher levels of posttraumatic distress and more somatic complaints in both the West Bank and Gaza regions. More Gaza than West Bank students reported symptoms meeting the criteria for PTSD, and more girls than boys in both groups reported somatic complaints. Thus, school-based screening can be an effective method for case identification of students showing PTSD symptoms as a result of exposure to political violence.

http://www.ptsd.va.gov/professional/newsletters/research-quarterly/v21n4.pdf

Abstract Elements

Use this list to help proofread your completed abstract.

Inspire your readers to read on with your research's value, complexity, and future results.

State the problem to be solved in clear discipline-specific terminology (explain unfamiliar terms.) Always remember to write complete sentences, employing action verbs. No reference to the author or document is necessary (DO NOT WRITE: Stanley Student wrote this abstract describing ...).

Explain the methodology applied in resolving the specific problem (analyses, samples, field data, variable controls, etc.).

Answer the question to be solved in clear terms; whereas, not to lead your readers astray.

State the implications of your answer given. Will your research be successfully accepted by the world, revolutionize the discipline area, or perhaps lead to unexpected changes?

Watch your word count limit. Journal editors provide set patterns that writers must adhere to when formulating abstracts. Condense a short paper of 2,000 – 5,000 words to approximately 100 – 250; reduce a longer paper, an article or book chapter of over 5,000 words to 250 or less; and a lengthy thesis or book may consist of about 300 words or less.

Key words are quite often requested by various publications and should appear with your abstract at the beginning of your paper. Closely follow the "Guidelines for Authors" per the number of key words accepted (quite often 3 – 10 words for indexing the article). Widespread use of these is for search listings, and your research papers may be assigned to review committees or editors.

Acronyms require explanation. At first mention in the abstract and footnotes, spell out the entire phrase followed by the acronym in parentheses. Subsequent mention of this topic may employ the acronym form. Remember to maintain consistency of acronyms throughout the abstract and article. For example: the American Medical Association (AMA)

Writing Academic Abstracts

An academic abstract highlights the fundamental ideas of a research paper. This is a writing that stands alone below the title. Make note: an abstract is NOT an introduction. After you complete writing your research paper, then, type the abstract in the same language as the original research plus one of the world languages. This text will suffice as a marketing tool in acquiring interested readers in your subject area.

Additionally, the abstract should logically parallel the original research text without adding any new information. Implement all strategies learned in unifying a paper coherently, concisely, and able to stand alone. The use of transitions is mandatory for steady flow throughout, along with all of the keywords. Since the abstract may be the most important part of your article, inclusion of these keywords is unquestionable.

Abstract content should include:

- **Introduction/Objective**: main objective research question (may include background information & problem statement hypothesis), pertinent literature evaluations.

- **Methods**: approach, research methodology.

- **Results**: main findings in solving problem and discussion.

- **Conclusions:** what the results mean and further points.

Abstracts must address:

- The problem elicited with background information.
- The resolution or future proposals.
- A sample showing the workings.
- An assessment: comparing present solutions/methods.

Finally, abstracts need to answer these questions:

- **What and why?**
- **What it is you exactly found?**
- **How you accomplished this?**

How to begin?

First, let us see some opening sentences that DO NOT offer real information:

1. *This paper describes an experiment for...*
2. *The paper investigates the idea of...*
3. *The reason for our study is to reflect on how...*
4. *The purpose of this research is to verify...*

As you can see, these openings are too general. One must proceed immediately to the main subject, awarding the reader with something solid in deciding to read further or not.

Second, let us see some sentences that DO offer real information:

Take a look at the following introductory sentences which go directly to the source; supplying the reader with a crystal clear vision of what the research is all about.

1. An interactive data management (IDM) system for the Spinal Cord Injury (SCI) Service has been developed to collect self-reported patient data related to secondary medical

166

complications and to provide feedback to the SCI rehabilitation team.

2. Kinematic aspects of the reduced shooting ability of tetraplegic (TP) wheelchair basketball players is investigated and compared with those of able-bodied (AB) basketball players.

3. Long-term exercise participation among older adults will result in healthier lifestyles and reduced need for health care.

http://www.rehab.research.va.gov/jour/02/39/1/abswalter.html
http://www.rehab.research.va.gov/jour/02/39/1/absNunome.htm
http://www.rehab.research.va.gov/jour/02/39/1/absBoyette.htm

Suggestions for clear, concise abstracts:

1. Type in the active voice, along with the third person singular.

2. Begin your abstract with a clearly focused introductory sentence written in the present verb tense.

3. It is common practice to use the past tense for work being described in the body.

4. Quite often earlier work is either written in the present or past tenses.

5. Aim for clarity by writing your first and last sentences in the present tense.

6. Keep your writing to only one paragraph.

7. Adhere to the specific number of words mandated by the publisher.

8. Answer: what, why, and how?

9. Use words that are common to the reader.

10. Use some keywords.

11. Utilize transitions between sentences.

12. Concluding statements must be written in the present tense: explaining the results. (e.g. *"These results mean..."*).

13. Proofread and edit grammar.

14. Refer to headings, subheadings and tables as guides.

15. Printout and reread aloud the abstract's hard copy.

16. Do not refer to sections of your paper.

17. Do not add literature references or graphics.

18. In no way, use acronyms.

19. Without a doubt, never insert any new information.

20. Unnecessary information should never be included.

21. By no means, incorporate your personal opinions.

22. Avoid redundancy.

23. Never repeat the article's heading.

Exercise 8-A

Each student will bring to class an abstract sample from their particular field of study for discussion and critique. If working on your own, you may search for abstracts on the Internet for self study.

Structured Abstracts

Using Structured Abstracts

A structured abstract stands apart from other abstracts with distinct, labeled sections (for example: Introduction, Methods, Results, Discussion) for rapid comprehension. Some disciplines prefer to use structured abstracts organized in outline format with sub-headings for each area of the abstract. Before using this style of abstract, check with your advisor/department to verify which style is preferred. The following are examples of such abstracts.

An evaluation of structured abstracts in journals published by the British Psychological Society

Hartley, J. and Benjamin, M. (1998), An Evaluation of Structured Abstracts in Journals Published by the British Psychological Society. *British Journal of Educational Psychology,* 68: 443–456. doi: 10.1111/j.2044-8279.1998.tb01303.x

Background. In 1997 four journals published by the British Psychological Society — the *British Journal of Clinical Psychology*, the *British Journal of Educational Psychology*, the *British Journal of Health Psychology*, and *Legal and Criminological Psychology* — began publishing structured abstracts.

Aims. The aim of the studies reported here was to assess the effectiveness of these structured abstracts by comparing them with original versions written in a traditional, unstructured, format.

Method. The authors of articles accepted for publication in the four journals were asked to supply copies of their original traditional abstracts (written when the paper was submitted) together with copies of their structured abstracts (when the paper was revised). 48 such requests were made, and 30 pairs of abstracts were obtained. These abstracts were then compared on a number of measures.

Results. Analysis showed that the structured abstracts were significantly more readable, significantly longer, and significantly more informative than the traditional ones. Judges assessed the contents of the structured abstracts more quickly and with significantly less difficulty than they did the traditional ones. Almost every respondent expressed positive attitudes to structured abstracts.

Conclusions. The structured abstracts fared significantly better than the traditional ones on every measure used in this enquiry. We recommend, therefore, that the editors of other journals in the social sciences consider adopting structured abstracts.

http://psychsource.bps.org.uk/details/journalArticle/3348651/An-evaluation-of-structured-abstracts-in-journals-published-by-the-British-Psych.html

Sample Structured Abstract

Current findings from research on structured abstracts

Hartley, J. (2004), Current findings from research on structured abstracts. Published by
the Journal of Medical Library Association, 2004 July; 92(3): 368–371.
PMCID: PMC442180

BACKGROUND:

Structured abstracts were introduced into medical research journals in the mid-1980s. Since then they have been widely used in this and other contexts.

AIM:

The aim of this paper is to summarize the main findings from research on structured abstracts and to discuss the limitations of some aspects of this research.

METHOD:

A narrative literature review of all of the relevant papers known to the author was conducted.

RESULTS:

Structured abstracts are typically longer than traditional ones, but they are also judged to be more informative and accessible. Authors and readers also judge them to be more useful than traditional abstracts. However, not all studies use "real-life" published examples from different authors in their work, and more work needs to be done in some cases.

CONCLUSIONS:

The findings generally support the notion that structured abstracts can be profitably introduced into research journals. Some arguments for this, however, have more research support than others.

http://www.ncbi.nlm.nih.gov/pmc/articles/PMC442180/

Sample

The following *structured abstracts* are formatted in lorem ipsum (nonsensical Greek serving as placeholders for text).

OBJECTIVE: Lorem ipsum dolor sit amet, consectetur adipisicing elit, sed do eiusmod tempor incididunt ut labore et dolore magna aliqua.

DESIGN: Lorem ipsum dolor sit amet, consectetur adipisicing elit, sed do eiusmod tempor incididunt ut labore et dolore magna aliqua. Ut enim ad minim veniam.

SETTING: Lorem ipsum dolor sit amet, consectetur adipisicing elit, sed do eiusmod tempor incididunt ut labore et dolore magna aliqua.

PARTICIPANTS: Lorem ipsum dolor sit amet, consectetur adipisicing elit, sed do eiusmod tempor incididunt ut labore et dolore magna aliqua. Ut enim ad minim veniam, quis nostrud exercitation ullamco laboris nisi ut aliquip ex ea commodo consequat.

RESULTS: Lorem ipsum dolor sit amet, consectetur adipisicing elit, sed do eiusmod tempor incididunt ut labore et dolore magna aliqua. Ut enim ad minim veniam, quis nostrud exercitation ullamco laboris nisi ut aliquip ex ea commodo consequat. Duis aute irure dolor in reprehenderit in voluptate velit esse cillum dolore eu fugiat nulla pariatur. Excepteur sint occaecat cupidatat non proident, sunt in culpa qui officia deserunt mollit anim id est laborum.

CONCLUSIONS: Lorem ipsum dolor sit amet, consectetur adipisicing elit, sed do eiusmod tempor incididunt ut labore et dolore magna aliqua. Ut enim ad minim veniam, quis nostrud exercitation ullamco laboris nisi ut aliquip ex ea commodo consequat. Duis aute irure dolor in reprehenderit in voluptate velit esse cillum dolore eu fugiat nulla pariatur.

KEYWORDS: ipsum; dolor; amet; consectetur; adipisicing; elit

(*Make note here, insert semi-colons between key words and capitalize only proper nouns.*)

Sample

GOAL: Lorem ipsum dolor sit amet, consectetur adipisicing elit.

PATIENTS AND METHOD: Lorem ipsum dolor sit amet, consectetur adipisicing elit, sed do eiusmod tempor incididunt ut labore et dolore magna aliqua.

RESULTS: Lorem ipsum dolor sit amet, consectetur adipisicing elit, sed do eiusmod tempor incididunt ut labore et dolore magna aliqua. Ut enim ad minim veniam, quis nostrud exercitation ullamco laboris nisi ut aliquip ex ea commodo consequat.

CONCLUSION: Lorem ipsum dolor sit amet, consectetur adipisicing elit, sed do eiusmod tempor incididunt ut labore et dolore magna aliqua. Ut enim ad minim veniam, quis nostrud exercitation ullamco laboris nisi ut aliquip ex ea commodo consequat. Duis aute irure dolor in reprehenderit in voluptate velit esse cillum dolore eu fugiat nulla pariatur. Excepteur sint occaecat cupidatat non proident, sunt in culpa qui officia deserunt mollit anim id est laborum.

KEYWORDS: lorem; ipsum; consectetur; adipisicing; eiusmod

*(**Make note here, insert semi-colons between key words and capitalize only proper nouns.**)*

http://loremipsum.net/

Using Structured Abstracts

Some disciplines prefer to use structured abstracts organized in outline format with sub-headings for each area of the abstract. Before using this style of abstract, check with your advisor/department to verify which style is preferred. The following are examples of such abstracts.

Abstract

BACKGROUND:

Structured abstracts were introduced into medical research journals in the mid 1980s. Since then they have been widely used in this and other contexts.

AIM:

The aim of this paper is to summarize the main findings from research on structured abstracts and to discuss the limitations of some aspects of this research.

METHOD:

A narrative literature review of all of the relevant papers known to the author was conducted.

RESULTS:

Structured abstracts are typically longer than traditional ones, but they are also judged to be more informative and accessible. Authors and readers also judge them to be more useful than traditional abstracts. However, not all studies use "real-life" published examples from different authors in their work, and more work needs to be done in some cases.

CONCLUSIONS:

The findings generally support the notion that structured abstracts can be profitably introduced into research journals. Some arguments for this, however, have more research support than others.

The following *structured abstracts* are formatted in lorem ipsum (nonsensical Greek serving as placeholders for text).

OBJECTIVE: Lorem ipsum dolor sit amet, consectetur adipisicing elit, sed do eiusmod tempor incididunt ut labore et dolore magna aliqua.

SCHEMA: Lorem ipsum dolor sit amet, consectetur adipisicing elit, sed do eiusmod tempor incididunt ut labore et dolore magna aliqua. Ut enim ad minim veniam.

SETTING: Lorem ipsum dolor sit amet, consectetur adipisicing elit, sed do eiusmod tempor incididunt ut labore et dolore magna aliqua.

PARTICIPATORS: Lorem ipsum dolor sit amet, consectetur adipisicing elit, sed do eiusmod tempor incididunt ut labore et dolore magna aliqua. Ut enim ad minim veniam, quis nostrud exercitation ullamco laboris nisi ut aliquip ex ea commodo consequat.

RESULTS: Lorem ipsum dolor sit amet, consectetur adipisicing elit, sed do eiusmod tempor incididunt ut labore et dolore magna aliqua. Ut enim ad minim veniam, quis nostrud exercitation ullamco laboris nisi ut aliquip ex ea commodo consequat. Duis aute irure dolor in reprehenderit in voluptate velit esse cillum dolore eu fugiat nulla pariatur. Excepteur sint occaecat cupidatat non proident, sunt in culpa qui officia deserunt mollit anim id est laborum.

CONCLUSIONS: Lorem ipsum dolor sit amet, consectetur adipisicing elit, sed do eiusmod tempor incididunt ut labore et dolore magna aliqua. Ut enim ad minim veniam, quis nostrud exercitation ullamco laboris nisi ut aliquip ex ea commodo consequat. Duis aute irure dolor in reprehenderit in voluptate velit esse cillum dolore eu fugiat nulla pariatur.

KEYWORDS: ipsum; dolor; amet; consectetur; adipisicing; elit

(Make note here, insert semi-colons between key words and capitalize only proper nouns.)

Structured Abstract

OBJECTIVE: Lorem ipsum dolor sit amet, consectetur adipisicing elit.

PATIENTS AND METHOD: Lorem ipsum dolor sit amet, consectetur adipisicing elit, sed do eiusmod tempor incididunt ut labore et dolore magna aliqua.

RESULTS: Lorem ipsum dolor sit amet, consectetur adipisicing elit, sed do eiusmod tempor incididunt ut labore et dolore magna aliqua. Ut enim ad minim veniam, quis nostrud exercitation ullamco laboris nisi ut aliquip ex ea commodo consequat.

CONCLUSION: Lorem ipsum dolor sit amet, consectetur adipisicing elit, sed do eiusmod tempor incididunt ut labore et dolore magna aliqua. Ut enim ad minim veniam, quis nostrud exercitation ullamco laboris nisi ut aliquip ex ea commodo consequat. Duis aute irure dolor in reprehenderit in voluptate velit esse cillum dolore eu fugiat nulla pariatur. Excepteur sint occaecat cupidatat non proident, sunt in culpa qui officia deserunt mollit anim id est laborum.

(Make note here, insert semi-colons between key words and capitalize only proper nouns.)

http://loremipsum.net/

Exercise 8-B

Abstract Revision Exercise

Before revising the sample abstract below, reflect on the 4 parts of an informative abstract.

- Objective/Introduction   (State motivation or main
                              purpose for the research study.)

- Methods   (Briefly explain the procedure
                              to validate the research.)

- Results   (Share highlighted observations
                              plus/or data gathered.)

- Conclusion   (Concisely assess the results.
                              Confirm or negate hypothesis.)

Consider the purpose of the abstract: academic readers will examine abstracts first; subsequently, if the material seems interesting, pertinent, and skillfully written, next, they will continue reading the article.

TOWARDS COMMON-SENSE REASONING
VIA CONDITIONAL SIMULATION:
LEGACIES OF TURING IN ARTIFICIAL INTELLIGENCE

CAMERON E. FREER, DANIEL M. ROY, AND JOSHUA B. TENENBAUM

Abstract. The problem of replicating the excitability of human common-sense reasoning has captured the imagination of computer scientists since the early days of Alan Turing's foundational work on computation and the philosophy of artificial intelligence. In the intervening years, the idea of cognition as computation has emerged as a fundamental tenet of Artificial Intelligence (AI) and cognitive science. But what kind of computation is cognition? We describe a computational formalism centered around a probabilistic Turing machine called QUERY, which captures the operation of probabilistic-conditioning via conditional simulation. Through several examples and analyses, we demonstrate how the QUERY abstraction can be used to cast common-sense reasoning as probabilistic inference in a statistical model of our observations and the uncertain structure of the world that generated that experience. This formulation is a recent synthesis of several research programs in AI and cognitive science, but it also represents a surprising convergence of several of Turing's pioneering insights in AI, the foundations of computation, and statistics.

Subjects: Artificial Intelligence (cs.AI); Logic (math.LO); Machine Learning (stat.ML)

http://arxiv.org/pdf/1212.4799.pdf, arXiv.org

1.   The **background**, "The problem of replicating the excitability of human common-sense reasoning has captured the imagination of computer scientists since the early days of Alan Turing's foundational work on computation and the philosophy of artificial intelligence. In the intervening years, the idea of cognition as computation has emerged as a fundamental tenet of Artificial Intelligence (AI) and cognitive science. But what kind of computation is cognition?"

2.   The **objective,** "We describe a computational formalism centered around a probabilistic Turing machine called QUERY, which captures the operation of probabilistic-conditioning via conditional simulation."

3.   The **methods,** "Through several examples and analyses, we demonstrate how the QUERY abstraction can be used to cast common-sense reasoning as probabilistic inference in a statistical model of our observations and the uncertain structure of the world that generated that experience."

4.   The **results,** "...we demonstrate how the QUERY abstraction can be used to cast common-sense reasoning as probabilistic inference in a statistical model of our observations and the uncertain structure of the world that generated that experience."

5.   The **conclusion,** "This formulation is a recent synthesis of several research programs in AI and cognitive science, but it also represents a surprising convergence of several of Turing's pioneering insights in AI, the foundations of computation, and statistics."

Now, review how the authors accomplished delivering the four parts of an informative abstract.

1.   Do you agree with how the author followed the format above? If not, rearrange the sentences' format.

2.   Revise the wording to be more concise with better flow. This abstract is comprised of 163 words; try to edit it down to fewer words.

Reduction of Wordiness to 140 words from 163

Abstract. Duplicating humans' excitability of common sense reasoning will never occur, but computer scientists' imaginations have been captured since Alan Turing's initial work on computation and artificial intelligence philosophy. Ever since that time, cognition has transformed into computation as a major theory of Artificial Intelligence (AI) and cognitive science. What kind of computation is cognition? We describe a computational formalism centered around a probabilistic Turing machine named QUERY, capturing the probabilistic-conditioning operation via conditional simulation. We demonstrate through several examples and analyses, how the QUERY abstraction can transmit common sense reasoning as probabilistic inference in a numeric observational model and the uncertain world structure that generated that experience. This formulation is a recent synthesis of several AI and cognitive science research programs. Also, it represents a surprising convergence of Turing's many pioneering insights in AI, the computational and statistical foundations.

Exercise 8-C

Now, it's your turn to reduce the wordiness of the original abstract. Cover the paragraph and reduce the number of words.

_____

_____

_____

_____

_____

_____

_____

_____

_____

Exercise 8-D

Organize the following sentences into proper order of the four main topics of an abstract.

- ❖ Introduction/Objective
- ❖ Methods
- ❖ Results
- ❖ Conclusion

Abstract

Writing Hindrance

____*Following this further, a graphic depiction illustrates students' scores segmented by specific categories of standard and non-standard English samples.*

____*In a non-hostile environment, second language learners were instructed to write a short essay on social media; subsequently, assessment of timed ESL writing samples proved this hypothesis.*

____*To sum up, given that formal academic writing is not easy for most ESL students, the results demonstrated that this additional hindrance manifested itself into a damaging habit. Future curriculums must acknowledge and address this problem in efforts to resolve it.*

____*Research has shown that second language learners are inundated with non-standard writing modes in social media which may hinder their academic writing.*

Key Words: non-standard English; social media; academic writing; standard English; second language learners

Abstract Writing Exercise

A Badly Written Abstract

Article Title: Architecture Capstone
Author: Anonymous

Abstract

This paper presents and assesses a framework for an architecture capstone design program for graduating senior undergraduate students. We give explanation on how student preparation, project selection, and teacher mentorship are the three key fundamentals that must be addressed prior to the capstone experience being ready for the students. Subsequently, we describe a way to oversee and carry out the capstone design experience including design workshops and lead architects. We describe the importance in assessing the capstone design experience and report recent assessment results of our framework. We comment specifically on what students thought were the most important aspects of their experience in architectural capstone design and provide measureable insight into what parts of the framework are most important.

Exercise 8-E

Critique:

(1) The introduction

(2) How the abstract is written in first, second, or third person.

(3) Results.

To review, elements of a good abstract generally contain:

(1) clear motivation for objective/s to be researched.

(2) methods.

(3) result evaluations and what they suggest (i.e., evidence, experimentation, statistics collection).

(4) meaning, vital to a high-quality abstract is inclusion of concrete and specific technical details motivating readers to discover more.

(5) how this research will benefit the domain.

(6) key words introduced.

Exercise 8-F

- After reading and critiquing this poorly written abstract above, label each sentence using the elements of a good abstract from the list above.

- Discuss how this abstract conforms or does not conform to the element criteria. (Some good abstracts may not entirely match the criteria.)

- Discuss how this could be improved.

A Well Written Abstract

Clin Psychol Rev. Author manuscript; available in PMC 2010 December 1.
Published in final edited form as:
Clin Psychol Rev. 2009 December; 29(8): 707–714.
Published online 2009 September 10. doi: 10.1016/j.cpr.2009.09.002
PMCID: PMC2783889
NIHMSID: NIHMS145157

Military-related PTSD and Intimate Relationships: from Description to Theory-Driven Research and Intervention Development

Candice M. Monson, Casey T. Taft, and Steffany J. Fredman

Abstract

Military operations in Iraq and Afghanistan have brought heightened awareness of military related PTSD, as well as the intimate relationship problems that accompany the disorder and can influence the course of veterans' trauma recovery. In this paper, we review recent research that documents the association between PTSD and intimate relationship problems in the most recent cohort of returning veterans and also synthesize research on prior eras of veterans and their intimate relationships in order to inform future research and treatment efforts with recently returned veterans and their families. We highlight the need for more theoretically-driven research that can account for the likely reciprocally causal association between PTSD and intimate relationship problems to advance understanding and inform prevention and treatment efforts for veterans and their families. Future research directions are offered to advance this field of study.

Keywords: PTSD; intimate relationship; couple; family; veterans; OEF/OIF; military

Introduction

Our military involvements in Iraq and Afghanistan, Operations Enduring Freedom and Iraqi Freedom (OEF/OIF), have raised awareness about the individual mental health consequences, such as posttraumatic stress disorder (PTSD) that can arise from traumatic stress exposure during the course of military deployment. At the same time, the scientific and lay communities have become more attuned to the family issues that surround a veteran when s/he returns with PTSD, as well as the individual and familial effects that are likely reciprocally related to the veteran's trauma recovery. This paper reviews recent research documenting the intimate relationship problems related to PTSD in OEF/OIF veterans and their intimate partners. We also synthesize research on prior eras of veterans and their intimate relationships and briefly review intervention efforts that have involved veterans' intimate partners. A next crucial step in advancing the study of veterans' PTSD and intimate relationship functioning is to develop and test theoretical models that can account for the well-established association between this individual psychopathology and relationship problems. We conclude the paper by reviewing these efforts and offering suggestions to improve the understanding and treatment of problems in both areas.

http://www.ncbi.nlm.nih.gov/pmc/articles/PMC2783889/

Critique:

(1) This abstract begins with a succinct statement of the problem and paper's objective: posttraumatic stress disorder (PTSD) and how it affects intimate relationships of military personnel returning home.

(2) The methods entailed research reviews of recently returned veterans' traumatic stress experienced; how their intimate relationships were impacted; and compared documented like situations of intervention.

(3) The results are aimed at apprising further study and treatment of returning veterans and their families. Future research instructions are offered to advance this field of study.

(4) The conclusion proposes advice for future study of comparable PTSD affecting these relationships. Subsequently, increase understanding, treat PTSD with associated challenges; and hopefully, alleviate this problem.

Exercise 8-G

ABSTRACT PARTS

↓
Introduction/Objective Explain the study's purpose.
↓
Methods Describe how the study commenced.
↓
Results Report the results that were found.
↓
Conclusion Conclude briefly Explain what is important and why

Read the sample abstract below. Using the box preceding this paragraph, classify the sentences corresponding to the given parts headlined in the box on page 188.

COST-EFFECTIVENESS OF SUBSTITUTING POULTRY LITTER FOR UREA IN COTTON PRODUCTION IN ALABAMA

Authors: A. Baiyee-Mbi, J. Befecadu, H. Jones, and C. Ready

Alabama A&M University, P.O. Box 1087, Normal, Alabama 35762

The fast growing Alabama poultry industry produces an enormous amount of poultry litter annually that needs to be disposed of in a timely and environmentally safe manner. One method of dealing with this problem is to use the mineralogically rich poultry litter to grow row crops such as cotton. The purpose of this study is to determine whether poultry litter is a cost effective substitute for urea in cotton production in Alabama. Linear programming is used for the analysis and sensitivity analysis is performed to determine the level of stability of the results in the basic models of the scenarios. The results of this study indicate that cotton fertilized with free fresh litter with a maximum of 100 miles transportation cost and purchased fresh litter with a maximum of 25 miles transportation cost had a higher income above variable cost (IAVC) than urea, hence a profitable substitute for urea in cotton production in Alabama. On the other hand, cotton fertilized with composted poultry litter had a lower IAVC at all levels than urea, hence not a profitable substitute for urea in cotton production. The optimal level of fresh litter, application that maximized the IAVC, is fresh litter providing 80 pounds of nitrogen per acre.

(http://www.nal.usda.gov/afsic/nsfc/pabstr.htm)

Sentence 1

Sentence 2

Sentence 3

Sentence 4

Sentence 5

Sentence 6

Sentence 7

Read this short article and write your own abstract.

Seasonal Affective Disorder

Posted January 25, 2011

While it may be just a temporary case of "winter blues" for most people, for others the long cold days of winter can be a serious psychological problem.

It's called Seasonal Affective Disorder – and never has an acronym been more apropos: SAD.

According to Dr. Joseph V. Pace, Chief of Psychiatry at the Alaska VA Medical Center, SAD is defined as "recurring depression with seasonal onset and remission."

Two seasonal patterns of SAD have been described: the fall-onset SAD and the summer-onset SAD. The fall-onset type, also known as "winter depression," is most recognized. In this subtype, major depressive episodes begin in late fall to early winter and decrease during summer months.

Dr. Pace adds that some of the symptoms of SAD include increased appetite, weight gain, sleep loss, decreased energy and lack of motivation.

He notes that, "Usually, we do not see pure seasonal depression, but seasonal worsening of pre-existing depression. Also, low vitamin D levels are common in our Alaskan vets and can correlate with depression. We screen for that and treat it."

One of the treatments he also recommends is aerobic exercise, "which can sometimes help."

The cause of SAD is not well understood. It is believed that the decreasing daylight available in fall and winter triggers a depressive episode in people predisposed to develop the disorder. However, no studies have established a causal relationship between decreasing daylight and the development of winter SAD.

One of the most effective remedies for dealing with the condition is light therapy. Light therapy has proven effective in a limited number of small, placebo-controlled studies.

The usual dose is 10,000 lux (the intensity of light that hits or passes through a surface) beginning with one 10-to-15 minute session per day, usually in the morning, gradually increasing to 30-to-45 minutes per day, depending upon response.

It may take four-to-six weeks to see a response, although some patients improve within days. Therapy is continued until sufficient daily light exposure is available through other sources, typically from springtime sun.

Light therapy is considered first-line therapy in patients who are not severely suicidal, have medical reasons to avoid antidepressant drugs, have a history of a positive response to light therapy, or if the patient specifically requests it.

Medication is also an option in some cases. Drugs may be a better option in patients with significant functional impairment or who are at high suicide risk, for patients with a history of moderate to severe recurrent depression and for patients who have had a prior positive response to antidepressants or mood stabilizers or who have failed other therapies.

Dr. Pace recommends that any Veterans experiencing unusual depression during the winter months should see their VA doctor as soon as possible.

By Hans Petersen, VA Staff Writer
http://www.mentalhealth.va.gov/featureArticle_Jan25SAD.asp

Practice Writing

Now, it is your turn to write your own abstract.

_____

_____

_____

_____

_____

_____

_____

_____

YOUR NOTES

SECTION 9

Research Papers
&
Delivering Speeches

Writing Process for Research Papers

(1) **Read the assignment sheet** carefully, highlighting requirements and paraphrasing the purpose. Reread the assignment sheet at each step of the writing process.

(2) **Find a workable topic** by consulting online indexes. Scan subheadings and article titles. Is there enough written on this topic? Do you have the background needed to write on this topic?

(3) **Familiarize yourself with the topic** by reading a few general online articles.

(4) Once you have some general knowledge about the topic, **formulate a possible thesis**. Think about questions that have come to mind as you read about the topic. Think of problems that need solving. Decide whether you should focus on convincing us that there is a problem or, if researchers agree that the problem exists, whether you should focus on solutions. You might want to write two possible theses and ask your instructor for input on which one seems more workable and interesting.

(5) **Develop a very broad outline** with a number for each section. Indicate how many pages you plan to devote to each section.

(6) **Research your thesis in depth**. Using your outline as a guide, decide how much material you will need for each section, and evaluate which sources are the best. Print your sources and read them, highlighting facts and quotations that you might want to use. For books, take notes in a notebook, being careful to record proper citations and page numbers of each source.

(7) After your initial reading, go through your source material again, reevaluating everything you highlighted or notated. If a note or highlighted sentence still seems important, use red ink to **write a number in the margin to correspond with a section of your outline**. Revise your outline if needed and continue revising even as you write the paper.

(8) Write the paper section by section, reading all appropriate sources just before writing a section. For example, before writing the third section of your paper, scan through your sources, rereading any highlighted material that you have labeled as "section three." Now, put your sources aside and write that section in your own words, looking back at a source only when you need to pull out a fact or quotation. If looking back at a source will get you off track, write XXX in the paper where a fact or quotation will be plugged in later. After you finish writing the section, go back to your sources to verify everything and/or plug in missing information. **This method of not looking at your sources as you write, will help you avoid writing a "cut and paste" paper**.

(9) Revise for clarity, accuracy, brevity, and relevance. Ask yourself the point of each paragraph and be able to express this in a single sentence. Check for plagiarism. Ask for feedback from the instructor, a fellow student, or a tutor.

(10) Proofread for grammar, punctuation, and missing documentation.

Writing Tip

When writing papers for courses, try waiting 2-3 days before submitting them. Then, proofread for the last time and see mistakes that need editing. At times, when everything is still fresh in one's mind after typing the paper's final draft, mistakes cannot be detected. When using this method, errors can be easily noticed.

A Word about Procrastination:

Be honest with yourself. If you have a tendency to put off writing a paper until the last possible minute, take steps to prevent that from happening again. The easiest method is to make an appointment with your professor to review your rough draft. Set the appointment a few days before the actual due date for the paper. This will help you finish writing your paper early – in time for your appointment rather than ten minutes before the paper is due.

University of Illinois (UIC) Academic Center for Excellence
2900 Student Services Building
http://www.uic.edu/depts/ace

Formal Outlines

Formal outlines are written to supply a broad plan for a paper's or speech's subject to be presented. All of the outline topics stem from the given subject and are related to one another. It is formatted as to the topics ordered as foremost and those succeeding. Quite often, chronological order may be a good choice. One of the most accepted outline forms is establishing a general topic and following with more specifics which support the topic. Here, we will be focusing on topic outlines which use single word headings or very brief phrases

Example

Take a look at the sample below and notice how a graduating system of numbers and letters with periods is set up per relative importance.

TOPIC OUTLINE

Hazardous Drivers

I. Different types

   A. Reckless

      1. Irresponsible

      2. Self-centered

      3. Dangerous

   B. Distracted

      1. Busy with cell phone

      2. Unaware of others

      3. Dangerous

II. Defensive driving

   A. Keep a safe distance

   B. Alert other driver

      1. Use horn

      2. Flash lights

There are two types of outlines (topic outline & sentence outline). Here, we are focusing on the topic outline which uses single words and/or very short phrases. Be sure that each heading and sub-heading has two or more topics below it. Within each part, your wording must be parallel word forms: nouns parallel with nouns, adjectives parallel with adjectives, etc. When it comes to your introduction and conclusion, it is not necessary to include these in your outline, but if you feel that it makes your outline stronger, by all means include it.

DETAILED OUTLINE FORM FOR SHORT PAPER

Title: _____

Introduction paragraph

The introduction begins with phrases to capture your reader's attention. Next, the statements are comprised of background information; culminating your first paragraph by writing the thesis statement with the main points to be covered. (about three for this sample)
This outline section is purely for visualization, but you may jot down notes on the lines.

Hook: _____

_____

Background: _____

_____

Thesis statement: _____

_____

Body paragraph 1

This body of writing begins with the first main point of your thesis statement. Then, continue writing sentences with information supporting this main point. As you write, remember to continuously refer back to this body's main idea so you do not lose focus. Always try to finish each body text with a conclusion that completes your objective.

Topic sentence: _____

_____

Support 1: _____

_____

Support 2: _____

_____

Support 3: _____

_____

Concluding sentence: _____

_____

Body paragraph 2

Here, you will address the second main point of your thesis; remember to utilize transitional phrases and words to allow your writing to flow smoothly as you introduce new information to readers. After writing supportive body content in a cohesive manner, finish up this text as previously with concluding comments.

Topic sentence: _____

_____

Support 1: _____

_____

Support 2: _____

_____

Support 3: _____

_____

Concluding sentence: _____

_____

Body paragraph 3

Lastly, you will focus on your final and third main point of your thesis. Before writing this fourth paragraph/section of your paper, scan through your sources, rereading any highlighted material that you have labeled as "section four." Now, put your sources aside and write that section in your own words, looking back at a source only when you need to pull out a fact or quotation. If looking back at a source will get you off track, write XXX in the paper where a fact or quotation will be plugged in later.

Topic sentence: _____

_____

Support 1: _____

_____

Support 2: _____

_____

Support 3: _____

_____

Concluding sentence: _____

_____

Concluding Paragraph

Continue on with body text in an organized fashion. When you have completed explaining all of the supportive information, begin work on your concluding paragraph. At this point, restate the paper's major points underscoring their importance. This information comes from your thesis statement, but be sure not to use the same exact wording from your introductory paragraph. Quite often, the last sentence of the concluding paragraph may suggest a future possibility related to your topic. You are the author, so create something of interest your readers may remember you.

Topic sentence: _____

_____

Sentence 1: _____

_____

Sentence 2: _____

_____

Sentence 3: _____

_____

Concluding Sentence: _____

_____

ORGANIZATION OF YOUR WRITING

Initially, an adequate understanding of the writing assignment is mandatory. After choosing a topic, the next step begins with brainstorming ideas related to the main idea. For instance, let's say your assigned topic is "Going Green," or taking care of our earth today and in the future to come. On a blank piece of paper, write Going Green in the center. As general thoughts come to mind, write them around your subject. You should be able to generate several new ideas using this informal method.

wind energy   recycle   economize   natural products

bring lunch to work   online bill pay   rechargeable batteries

global warming   ***Going Green***   solar energy

conserve energy   share   fuel efficiency   vegetarian

plant trees   purchase gently used items   telecommute   donate

stay home nightly   timers   fluorescent lights   online accounting

pollution   environment

Be sure and write as many ideas as possible. Then, eliminate those that do not meet your requirements. The next step is organizing your ideas into outline form. Separate information into different categories.

Going Green

I. <u>Global Efforts</u>	II. <u>Work Related Efforts</u>	III. <u>Personal Efforts</u>
wind energy	online accounting	recycle
global warming	share rides	economize
solar energy	efficiency	natural products
conserve energy	recycle	online bill pay
fuel efficiency	telecommuting	rechargeable items
forestation	fluorescent lights	conserve energy
pollution	timers	share
environment	public transportation	vegetarian
		forestation
		fuel efficiency
		purchase gently used items
		donate
		fluorescent lights
		timers

You may organize your paper in the following manner.

- Section 1 may be devoted to helping our earth go green with global efforts.
- Section 2 can center on work related efforts.
- Section 3 may focus on humans' personal efforts.

Going Green *(working outline)*

I. Globally

> wind energy
>
> global warming
>
> solar energy
>
> conserve energy
>
> fuel efficiency
>
> forestation
>
> environment
>
> pollution

II. Work Related

> online accounting
>
> share rides
>
> efficiency
>
> recycle
>
> telecommuting
>
> fluorescent lights
>
> timers
>
> public transportation

III. Personal

> recycle   share
>
> economize   vegetarian
>
> natural products   forestation
>
> online bill pay   fuel efficiency
>
> rechargeable items   purchase gently used items
>
> conserve energy   donate

My thesis statement for "Going Green" might read as such:

*In sustaining our mother earth, "going green" involves
global, work-related, and personal levels of involvement.*

Subsequently, I suggest you begin *free writing* the text of the paper. This is a pre-writing method that allows you to freely write without attention to correct grammar, spelling, and sentence structure. Here, you are utilizing your brainstormed vocabulary to create a preliminary text; liberating you of mixed feelings you may have about your writing abilities. For now, do not worry about the mechanics of writing; simply express your thoughts on paper by the use of whatever methods you have found to work well. Later, you will revise according to proper academic style.

Exercise 9-A

Let's say, you choose a topic for brainstorming. Below, write a topic of interest in the center. As general thoughts come to mind, write them around your subject. You should be able to generate several new ideas using this informal method.

Be sure and write as many ideas as possible. Then, eliminate those that do not meet your requirements.

Writing an Outline

The next step is organizing your ideas into outline form. Separate information into different categories.

(working outline)

ARRANGING YOUR PAPER'S BODY

As you know, your paper begins with the introduction and culminates with a conclusion. Thus, it will be necessary to organize the order of your body paragraphs and/or sections. The following are general areas on how to order the sequence.

Increasing & decreasing importance: Here, you may choose to "hook" your readers with the strongest point and successively work down to the weakest point. Otherwise, the opposite order may work better for you; going from the weakest point, making your way ever stronger, and concluding with the most important item of interest. These transitions will help you convey ideas of importance.

additionally	*in addition to*	*moreover*	*furthermore*
	in fact *actually* *as a matter of fact*	*indeed*	
especially	*notably* *particularly*	*in particular*	*therefore*

Chronological: Using this arrangement method focuses on time and when things occur. The paper might involve the explanation of a progression or even the steps to something. Use transitional change words and phrases in separating sections of a paragraph.

first... second... third...

generally... furthermore... finally

in the first place... also... lastly

basically...similarly...as well

in the first place...pursuing this further...finally

to be sure...additionally...lastly

in the first place...just in the same way...finally

Additionally, sequence of time transitions are appropriate to use here.

after	*in the first place*	*finally*
afterwards	*in the meantime*	*before long*
as soon as	*later*	*then*
at first	*meanwhile*	
at last	*next*	
before	*soon*	

Compare & contrast:

In this situation it is important to logically guide your reader as to comments expressed to compare your topic or comments to contrast your topic. One way of handling this is to separate your paragraphs into similarities (comparisons) and differences (contrasts). Therefore, each paragraph only discusses one similarity or one difference. If you do choose to discuss all similarities together or all differences together, use phrases to guide your readers "an additional similarity…" or "another difference…" When discussing both similarities and differences together, make sure to use transitions like "in contrast" or "alternatively" to signal change in reasoning.

Definition:

As we have previously reviewed in Section 5 (Paragraph Level Definitions), a paper may be based on a term (topic) defined by placing that term within the class of objects or concepts to which the term belongs and then detailing all the unique traits that distinguish it from all others of its class. Such definitions are often *expanded* in academic, business, and technical writing by the use of graphics, examples, analogies, history, and citations.

Classification:

Your body text will be divided into key groups and differentiate between the groups by explaining your reasons for choosing these categories.

Cause and effect:

When a major causal relationship between items is your main point of the paper, separate each text paragraph by cause and then effect. Otherwise, you may choose the route of discussing causes and effects within a different style. Just remember to guide your reader with signposts (transitions), so no one "gets lost" inside your words.

Exercise 9-B

Write a Thesis Statement

Referring to your working outline that you have completed, write a thesis statement describing the main points of your research paper. You may look back at Section 7, thesis statements.

_____

_____

_____

_____

Now, write your introductory paragraph. Begin with a sentence that grabs the reader's attention. Next, write a couple of sentences giving background information on your topic. Finally, use your thesis statement from above as your last sentence in this paragraph.

_____

_____

_____

_____

_____

_____

_____

Congratulations! You have just written the first introductory paragraph of your research paper.

Exercise 9-C

Focus on the first main point of your thesis topic from exercise 9-B. Continue writing your second paragraph with information supporting this topic. As you write, remember to continuously refer back to the body's main idea so you do not lose focus. Always try to finish each body text with a conclusion that completes your objective.

_____

_____

_____

_____

_____

_____

_____

_____

Congratulations! You have just completed writing the second paragraph of your research paper.

Exercise 9-D

Here, you will address the second main point of your thesis; remember to utilize transitional phrases and words to allow your third paragraph to flow smoothly as you introduce new information to readers. After writing supportive body content in a cohesive manner, finish up with concluding comments to this third paragraph.

_____

_____

_____

_____

_____

_____

_____

Congratulations! You have just written the third paragraph of your research paper.

Exercise 9-E

Here, you will address the third main point of your thesis. Write this paragraph from everything you have researched in your own original words. You may look back at a source when you need to pull out a fact or quotation. After writing supportive body content in a cohesive manner, finish up with concluding comments to this fourth paragraph.

_____

_____

_____

_____

_____

_____

_____

_____

_____

Congratulations! You have just written the fourth paragraph of your research paper.

Exercise 9-F

Writing your Concluding Paragraph/Section

When you have completed explaining all of the supportive information, begin work on your concluding paragraph. At this point, restate the paper's major points underscoring their importance. This information comes from your thesis statement, but be sure not to use the same exact wording from your introductory paragraph. Quite often, the last sentence of the concluding paragraph may suggest a future possibility related to your topic. You are the author, so create something of interest your readers may remember you.

_____

_____

_____

_____

_____

_____

_____

_____

_____

Congratulations! You have just written the fifth and last paragraph/section of a sample research paper. Now, you should have a complete example to refer to when writing papers in the future.

ESTABLISHING YOUR OWN RESEARCH SPACE

In order to be accepted and recognized in today's world of academia, it is suggested that a novice start out by "voraciously digesting" past and present research in your chosen area of study. Next, when you have decided upon an area of focus, always credit prior research as valid and commendable. Subsequently, you may follow a line of investigation challenging prior studies. It may require filling a void and/or broadening the research area. Your new, fresh approach just may be what the field has been awaiting. Once you have found an area that requires such attention, seize it! Own it! Once you lay claim to it, cultivate this research space with everything you have. Consequently, take ownership of your own research space and be proud to study it, explore all the future opportunities, and enjoy your life's work!

1. In compiling an introduction, primarily state previous research and/or colleague's work as background information. Here, you may want to indicate new trends or other related areas of interest.

2. Secondarily, it may be appropriate to introduce your individual work as filling a gap or furthering earlier research in a novel approach.

3. As you fulfill your new role in bringing vital research to the community, your public will expect the rationale for your studies outlined. Be mindful of upholding your distinctive hypotheses, discoveries, and magnitude of your research.

Delivering Speeches

Why?

You may ask yourself, why do I need to deliver effective speeches? Well, your life's journey has guided you towards a life of research, be it in the area of academics, business, engineering, and/or medicine, just to name a few. This industrious research that you toil at must be shared with others interested in such work. Thus, where there is a will, there is a way. Since English is not your first language, public speaking may seem challenging. Plus, our world has become increasingly smaller in terms of the Internet; the English language is developing into one of the prime world languages of communication. Your personal success and that of your business, depends on you communicating clearly when presenting your diligent work. Your public awaits your accomplishments and speeches to enlighten them!

Organization

Good organization of your speech before delivery employs an outline, enabling the audience to easily follow along. Always include a thesis statement to inform the audience of the main idea of your chosen topic, use transitions as pointers when introducing a new idea or changing focus. When presenting your research; at all times, cite your resources precisely. Choose a format of organizing your outline in order to clearly stay on topic and allow your audience to easily follow along with your argument/statement. There are five popular formats: ***topical, chronological, spatial, cause-effect, and problem-solution sequence.***

Outline Rules

- Subdivide topics by a formation of Roman numerals and letters, followed by a period.

Example:

Thesis Statement:

I.
   A.
   B.
      1.
      2.
         a.
         b.
II.
   A.
   B.

- Both headings and subheadings should have at least two parts (i.e.: I. & II., A. & B.).
- Consistency is crucial. When using a topical outline; for instance, do not make use of whole sentences. Since this is an outline structured with topics, simply type brief phrases. First, the most frequently used format is the *topical.* For instance, when your thesis statement declares, "There are four Chicago weather seasons: spring, summer, fall, and winter." This would lead to four different sections within the body of your speech for each season, highlighting each season as an individual topic. Also within the topical format, the pro-con (advantages versus disadvantages) organization could also be utilized in comparing and contrasting main points. For example, II. B. could begin with the statement, "Summer advantages in Chicago far outweigh winter disadvantages in this fair city."

SAMPLE   **Topic Outline**

Topic: Chicago's Seasons

**Attention Getter
(Hook):**_____

Thesis Statement: There are four Chicago weather seasons: spring, summer, fall, and winter.

I. Introduction

          A. Definition of topic
          B. Significance of study
          C. Definition of terms

II. Body

          A. Chicago's spring
          B. Chicago's summer
          C. Chicago's fall
          D. Chicago's winter

III. Conclusion

          A. Conclusion (restatement of thesis in different words)
          B. Recommendations, summary
          C. Future or insightful question

Second, *chronological* organizing uses time for ordering proposals to your listeners. An example might entail your thesis presenting the past, present, and future progression of your topic. Your thesis statement may focus on, "The AIDS epidemic is of notable interest when considering the past, present, and future of this disease and its proposed treatments."

Sample   Chronological Outline

Topic: The Epidemiology of AIDS

Attention Getter (Hook):

_____

Thesis Statement: The AIDS epidemic is of notable interest when considering the past, present, and future of this disease and its proposed treatments.

I. Introduction

> A. Definition of topic
> B. Significance of study
> C. Definition of terms

II. Body

> A. 1980s: 2 significant events
> B. 1990s: 2 significant events
> C. 2000–2012: 2 significant events
> D. Future

III. Conclusion

> A. Restatement of thesis statement in different words
> B. Recommendations, summary
> C. Optimistic future or insightful question

Third, *spatial* ordering takes into consideration different areas. A thesis may be presented with different global areas of AIDS and the impact on these regions. Your thesis may state, "The AIDS virus has notably progressed through the African continent when considering different impacts on the north, central, and southern regions."

Sample   **Spatial Outline**

Topic: AIDS' Impact on African Regions

Attention Getter (Hook):

_____

Thesis Statement: The AIDS virus has notably progressed through the African continent when considering different impacts on the north, central, and southern regions.

I. Introduction

        A. Definition of topic
        B. Significance of study
        C. Definition of terms

II. Body

        A. Impact on northern Africa
        B. Impact on central Africa

III. Conclusion

        A. Restatement of thesis statement in different words
        B. Recommendations, summary
        C. Future or insightful question

Fourth, **cause-effect** is another organization method in order to present a clear connection linking theories. One would consider using this approach when speaking about good health maintenance, for example. The thesis statement could read as, "The effects of a good exercise regimen, weight control, and sleep hygiene can all contribute to a healthy long life." All of these positive effects on the body will cause a human being to enjoy a fit, extended life.

Sample   **Cause-Effect Outline**

Topic: Good Health Maintenance

Attention Getter (Hook):

Thesis Statement: The effects of a good exercise regimen, weight control, and sleep hygiene can all contribute to a healthy long life.

I. Introduction
        A. Definition of topic
        B. Significance of study
        C. Definition of terms
II. Body
        A. Causes of poor health maintenance
           1. No exercise, out of shape
           2. Overeats, wrong food
           3. Not sleeping well

        B. Effects of these causes
           1. Fat, little energy
           2. Overweight
           3. Tired, unclear thinking
III. Conclusion
        A. Restatement of thesis statement in different words
        B. Recommendations, summary
        C. Future or insightful question

Fifth, the ***problem-solution*** sequence is offered as a persuasive speech; convincing the audience of your solution to a problem. Let's say that you must address the topic of personal security at your university, a thesis statement may state, "Campus security relies on student vigilance after dark suggesting the buddy system, not displaying cell phones, and notifying campus police of any crimes." Your outlined speech would proceed to describe in detail how to solve the problem of campus crime.

Sample   **Problem-Solution Outline**

Topic: University Personal Security

Attention Getter (Hook):

Thesis Statement: Campus security relies on student vigilance after dark suggesting the buddy system, not displaying cell phones, and notifying campus police of any crimes.

I. Introduction
    A. Definition of topic
    B. Significance of study
    C. Definition of terms

II. Problems – Campus crime
    A. Crimes against university students
    B. Cell phone thefts
    C. Heightened awareness

III. Solutions – Student vigilance
    A. Buddy system after dark
    B. Hide cell phones
    C. Notification of crimes to campus police

IV. Conclusion
    A. Restatement of thesis statement in different words
    B. Recommendations, summary
    C. Future or insightful question

It is an excellent idea to have media with a projector and screen to illustrate your outline and paper copies to distribute to your audience. This way, they may follow along easily and appreciate your method of organization. Keep this outline very simple and concise with an easy to read type font and large point size.

If you plan on using handouts, it's best to distribute these to your listeners before your speech.

Past, Present, Future Speech Game

This fun game will ease your anxiety while allowing you to personally experience giving a speech. Each one of you needs to bring to our next class 3 things that represent the past, present, and future for you. The outline you will be creating will be based on the chronological outline example.

Example A: You may bring in a French book, American flag, and diploma. The French book represents your homeland where you grew up. The American flag signifies the country you are presently living and studying. The diploma is the reward you will receive in the future for all of your hard work.

Example B: You may bring in 3 items that have monetary significance (Chinese RMB, American dollar, and a bank statement). The Chinese RMB symbolizes the currency you used growing up in China. Our American dollar is the present form of money that you use. In the future, the bank statement is all you will see of your hard earned cash (and eventually paper statements will cease to exist, making way for e-statements).

This game will help you organize your thoughts in outline form before presenting to our class. Your outline should contain a simple thesis sentence. For example, "Currency forms have been changing throughout my life, and the future will offer computer-generated money." While giving your speech please do not forget to use transitions between major points, so everything flows well. Such as, "In the past when I was very young in China, I received Chinese RMBs from my grandparents during our spring festival. It seemed like so much money to me, but not today in America where I spend the bills quicker than deposits make it to the bank."

Evaluate Your Audience

Take into consideration your listeners' particular population, mindset, and uniqueness that they bring to your lecture. Be sure to find out as much as possible about their domestic and/or international status and their backgrounds as a whole. By adapting to their particular needs, your speech will take on a unique level of interest that each audience will relish in knowing you have gone out of your way to personally address them. Presently, our audiences are comprised of a multitude of cultural backgrounds. Therefore, always be cognizant of differences and expectations, so as not to offend anyone. Just as Christmas and New Years are holidays celebrated in the United States by closing schools, offices, stores, and factories, many others observe occasions from their cultural backgrounds. This may cause close perusal of a calendar or holiday listing; whereby, avoiding schedule conflicts of your speaking engagement.

Before your presentation begins, inform your audience on how you will take their questions (either during your speech or at the end). Most speakers prefer to take audience questions at the end of their speeches. Aim to deliver your information in a conversational tone of voice. For the most part, presenters prefer developing this tone since the audience members are most likely colleagues of yours, either one way or another. Confidently, you will pique their interest when delivering your information at this conversational tone. After your speech, try to attain feedback from your colleagues. Remember, this is constructive criticism that you may be able to incorporate into any upcoming speeches. Beware, always practice your speech as much as needed per the time allotted to your topic. During professional conventions, meetings, symposiums, etc., the organizing powers of the event must keep strict time limits for each presentation. Most likely, you may be asked to leave the podium if your time is up.

How to Begin with an Introduction

Move toward the podium at a normal pace of walking with good posture, self-assurance and, if so, smile to greet the audience. Definitely, make eye contact with as many people in the audience as possible. This serves as somewhat of a "handshake" with each attendee. Take some deep breaths to calm yourself before beginning to speak. Begin addressing the audience with a greeting, such as: Thank you, Good morning, or anything else that is appropriate. Be sure to deliver your name, pronouncing it in a slow manner and annunciating very clearly so everybody understands perfectly well. Do not make mention of how nervous you may be nor any jokes on that subject. Just go along with the flow as the audience perceives you as an experienced lecturer glowing with poise and direction. Bringing your energy to this arena forces you to center on your audience and the message you have to deliver. There is no room for self-consciousness.

In order to hook the attention of your audience, you will have less than a minute. As previously mentioned in our paraphrasing section, your introduction should attract the attention of your audience; making them eager to learn the answer, be hooked, and enticed to listen to your speech. You may begin with asking a question that does not even require an answer. For example: If man was designed to hunt and gather, then why are we sitting and staring at computer screens? You may even opt for a shocking statistic regarding the world-wide economy. Lastly, a brief but notable quotation related to your topic may be the perfect temptation for hooking your audience.

Body Language

The manner in which you hold your body can improve your image and the subject at hand. Always stand erect with good posture, a smile is appreciated by audiences, and speak confidently so that all attendees are able to hear you. You must articulate your words, so there is no confusion in what you are communicating. Be sure not to speak too quickly and try to pause at times. Never race through a speech because of nerves. By all means, do not read your report to the audience! They have taken the time to come and hear about your research. It will be much easier for them to understand about your studies if you just converse with them. You will be able to think more clearly, and the audience will benefit from following your clear line of reason. If you want to highlight something, simply pause before the item and a brief pause afterwards will shed light on this as significant. Maintain good eye contact for a few seconds each with as many people as possible. Last, but not least, move around while talking and try to be a bit animated by using your hands when speaking.

Visual Aids

If you plan on using visual aids, make sure that all of your equipment is in tip-top condition. Arrive early to the designated lecture hall and have a practice run with the audio-visual people employed there. Use common sense when adding visuals to your presentation, not too many, but just enough. When using this equipment, always remember to keep facing the audience (no display of your backside is necessary). Expect the unexpected. For example, the equipment may malfunction. Always be prepared.

Practice

Above all - remember to practice, practice, practice! Practice makes perfect! Before delivering your speech, rehearse it like you know the back of your hand! Have a friend observe you giving your speech and ask him/her for constructive criticism on your speech and body language.

Good luck!

SECTION 10

Critiques

How to Write Critiques

When assigned to write a critique on a given writing, professors are asking you to analyze and evaluate the text within your own opinioned mind. For that reason, *how, why,* and *how well* are answered in the critique. While interpreting, scrutinizing, and assessing the content, honestly pen your reaction after reading. Although we may relate the word critique to criticizing negatively, this is not necessarily the case. You may relate your reaction as positive, negative, or mixed. It's imperative to clarify the reasons why you responded in such a way to the writing.

While reading the article or book to be critiqued, keep in mind these analytical questions and jot down notes as you continue:

> ➢ the author's main idea
> ➢ the author's main objective
> ➢ the audience
> ➢ arguments author employs to support the main idea
> ➢ evidence author offers in support of arguments
> ➢ author's fundamental hypotheses or preconceived notions

Upon completion of reading the material, you can concentrate on evaluating the text, ask yourself the following:

> ➢ Are the arguments reasonable?
> ➢ Does the author present correct facts?
> ➢ Are important terms well defined?
> ➢ Is there enough evidence to substantiate the arguments?
> ➢ Is the writing suitable for the proposed audience?
> ➢ Are pros and cons offered?
> ➢ Does the text improve your understanding of the subject?
> ➢ Are there any areas that stimulate a significant response from you? If so, make note of them and your specific reaction.
> ➢ Think back on how you have been influenced by the topic. Has this writing swayed you one way or the other?
> ➢ What queries and/or opinions does this text bring to mind?

Now, it's time to begin planning your critique by introducing, summarizing, and assessing the text. Write in standard essay form, beginning with the introduction identifying the subject and your personal opinion. Be sure to defend your views by highlighting detailed concerns toward the arguments.

> Firstly, give explanation as to the author's ideas. Incorporate some of the specific sentences supporting the given viewpoints.
> Propose your own opinions on the arguments, while detailing points of agreement and disagreement.
> Summarize, quote, or paraphrase specific textual excerpts providing evidence for your opinions.
> Clarify how this text supports your opinions.

Your conclusion will reiterate your argument along with restating your opinions.

Guidelines in arranging your book review may encompass the following:

> an overview of the book by large sections or chapters which may lay a foundation for the subject; depict prospective readers; portray the authors; generalize on the subject matter and/or position the book in the particular field of study

> and/or - general and specific assessments (highlight positive and negative important points from each chapter and/or section plus graphics)

> and/or - the book's significance and its impact on the particular field of study

> and/or – some type of suggestions or approval (including deficiencies)

> and/or – commentary on the book's production (paper, ink, recyclability, binding, size and availability in electronic versions).

231

Writing Critiques

When composing written critiques, one should be unbiased and considerate. Your individual field of study generally requires differing terms of meaning for critiques. Therefore, you must be cognizant of criteria being unbiased in one area of study as opposed to another field, whereby, the same is considered biased. Additionally, diverse disciplines may emphasize differing topics in the critique. For example, in sociology, the critique may emphasize the methodology while nursing may stress the results and given implications on health.

Granted, book reviews dominate the critiques assigned in the social sciences. Unfortunately, for the international student, this may mean a hefty assignment of reading several books during the semester. Yet, there surely is a positive end result leaving you with a bank of evaluative language, hedging skills (cautiously avoiding an issue in a polite style), and intellectual prowess in your field of study. Concurrently, graduate students will learn how to assimilate these new readings with prior books through contrast. As well, these students will derive a keen sense of academic text in their field.

Writing Tip
Internet search engines can be used to help with vocabulary. If you are not sure how to use an English word in your text, simply look for it using a search engine. By that way, the word can be displayed in various contexts, so one is able to view how it is used appropriately.

ASSORTED ADJECTIVES USED IN EVALUATIVE LANGUAGE

<u>Positive</u>		<u>Negative</u>	
ambitious	impressive	simple	*evident
competent	complex	restricted	fleeting
descriptive	comprehensive	*atypical	gross
essential	practical	limited	intimidating
innovative	detailed	small	irritating
valuable	up-to-date	*careful	lacking
noteworthy	insightful	traditional	lightweight
explanatory	significant	preliminary	misguided
motivated	remarkable	*complex	outdated
astonishing		reticent	repetitious
ground-breaking		blemished	rushed
inspiring		narrow	scatter
appealing		substandard	tedious
well-designed		*unusual	time-consuming
useful		*modest	vague
important		flawed	brief
interesting		small scale	confusing
detailed		unsatisfactory	*coy
timely		difficult	cumbersome
clear		inconsistent	dangerous
accessible		lengthy	doubtful
exploratory		misleading	*elementary
significant		absent	extreme

*May be used as both positive and negative.

When expressing opinions in critiques, a useful technique positions opposite adjectives "to soften the blow" of criticism.

For example:

1. Although this article utilized an *overabundant* number of technical terms, it was still *lacking* in ...

2. Needless to say, the data here is *timely,* yet the *outdated* ...

3. The author's synopsis is commendable for its *detailed* description, but at times, it seemed quite *scattered* ...

4. This *time-consuming* review could have expressed the same ideas in a *clear, concise* manner while maintaining the original concepts of the research.

5. Smith's *modest* critique still offered *ground-breaking* data that must be pursued by others in our field.

6. Even though this *preliminary* text may seem substandard, it is still *useful* in the research arena of our discipline today.

7. The writer's article is *clearly ambitious*, nonetheless the *cumbersome...*

8. While Zenner's writing demonstrates a *limited perspective*, the findings *appear to be insightful* ...

Exercise 10-A

Beginning Phrases for Your Critique

The following are beginning phrases to spark your imaginative mind into writing critiques. Fill in the blanks with your own information.

- The following research by_____,(authors'
  names) presents a comprehensive, if not always tenable
  (reasonable) analysis of _____ in the article
  _____.

- In order to introduce the research topic,
  _____, (authors' names) study is a textbook
  example of ...

- _____(authors' names) have had a

  profound influence on ...

- This article, _____, by
  _____(authors' names) contains a
  number of new and important insights: ...

- The author's _____claim that ... is
  not well founded.

- The study offers only cursory (brief, quick) examinations of...

SAMPLE CRITIQUES

The following samples will give you a nice example of critiques.

#1

Distinguished Lecture Critique

Title: Designing Technologies for Learning: The Move from Cognitive Science to Anthropology

by Michael Eisenberg – University of Colorado at Boulder

February 16, 2012

Critique by Priscilla Jimenez

The goal of Michael Eisenberg's talk was to motivate the use of an anthropological approach instead of the well-known cognitive approach when designing technology for learning. Therefore, this talk reached a multidisciplinary community, researchers from computer science and learning sciences.

He started introducing his work (at The Craft Technology Group) and other related work. His work was mainly related to integrating educational technology into teaching and placing novel technology in the hands of children which enable them to build physical things. "Craft design tools", "Novel fabrication devices", and "Computationally enriched crafts" were the slide titles that clearly presented what he does. Each one of these slides showed a set of images that clarified its title. The presenter made a proper choice of images because these clearly explained and supported the speaker's intentions. However, during the talk, he mentioned some technologies and artifacts such as: lilypad and arduino, that might not be familiar with all the attendees. It would have been better to have them written on the slides. Also, he made transitions between slides full of images and slides full of text. A set of images with few words in the first slides would have been a smoother transition.

As this was not a presentation on a specific research work or solution, but a presentation of an approach that they are considering now to design and build new technology, he introduced the literature that inspires his work. His intention was to tell the audience and inspire the ones working in similar areas to consider this approach as well. Thus, the subsequent slides presented new themes or prospective areas, which were derived from ethnology/anthropology and could be explored to design technology for learning. They included an overview of different ideas, such as: programmable cards (computational collectibles); children's rooms as targets of design; programmable art to show in suburban houses; designing technology to use in specific holidays and creating technologies that facilitate making good friends. All the points shown in the slides were clear and supported by literature findings. The slides were simple and easy to follow. However, in the middle of the presentation he started showing some videos about projects they had built. I would suggest showing the videos at the beginning (in his work introduction) then mentioning them again in this part as an example of the new applied approaches. Another option could have been to finish talking about these potential areas to explore and after that, give a detailed explanation of the current projects.

The language and the presentation content were proper for a general audience. The presenter kept a good pace during the presentation. The timing was perfect. At the end, the speaker had time for answering questions, which were well addressed.

Finally, his speaking style was good. It kept my attention through the presentation. He spoke clearly, calm and facing the audience. He looked very comfortable too. Overall, the presentation was well organized, and the speaker delivered the central message. He tried to explain in detail his examples and new approaches. As it was mentioned before, the selected images were very good and accomplished its purpose.

SAMPLE CRITIQUE- #2
Faculty Candidate Talk
Title: Security and Reliability for Internet-Scale Services
by Phillipa Gill - PhD. Candidate at University of Toronto
Critique by Priscilla Jiménez

Phillipa Gill's talk focused on her current research. Her talk was related to challenges encountered on Internet routing security and reliability on network data centers (focusing on popular online services). She briefly covered important factors about data center reliability that was found in an empirical study she performed. Her research interests focused on network measurement, data analysis and ideas from economics to improve security and reliability of networks. She has spent time in well-known research labs such as: Microsoft, AT&T, and Boston University. Consequently, her work and publication history is impressive for being a young researcher (starting in 2007). She has written papers that have been influential and interesting for her research community.

Her presentation started with a good introduction of the topic. She utilized a graph to make clear the network current situation and to visualize the potential problem and challenges. Also, she mentioned a set of important real events that have happened around the world that demonstrated the unreliability of networks and Internet. She used many graphs (network representations) in her slides, which were consistent in the whole presentation (same images and colors). Those graphs were dynamically updated to clearly point out what she wanted to address. This made her slides easy to follow.

After presenting the current scenario, problems and challenges on the Internet and networks, she displayed a slide with a list of her contributions. This was a good transition. In this kind of presentation, it is important to show the audience the specific and individual contributions. In this list, she highlighted and grouped the ones that she was going to talk about in this specific presentation. For each of these papers, she presented the problem, the challenge and her approach. It was clear and well stated. Until this point, the flow of the slides was good. Then she started presenting an outline of the presentation every time she made a transition. It would have been better if she had continued without the outline. Additionally, although the slides were consistent in format and had a good appearance, she sometimes presented text that was difficult to see.

During and after the presentation, she received questions that she addressed very well. The language and the presentation content were proper for a computer science community. The presenter kept a good pace during the presentation. The timing was well managed too. Her speaking style was good. It kept my attention through the presentation. She spoke clearly, calm and facing the audience. She looked confident as she was presenting but sometimes she looked to the audience giving the impression that she nervously expected questions. Overall, the presentation was well organized and the speaker delivered the central message. The audience was attentive and asking questions, which is a sign that they were interested in what she was presenting. At the end, she also mentioned the future research that she wants to do. That was a good way to finish the talk.

Critiquing an Article

Quite often, graduate students are asked to critique an article from a journal within their specific field of study. At this point, the student must take on the role as a specialist in the given discipline. Fortunately, an article most likely will focus on a particular research dilemma and/or query. Depending on your subject area, common research questions may be asked. As with engineering, the conclusions may not adequately support the original question posed; therefore, you would pursue this by offering additional testing methods and/or more proof. Health research articles adhere to the Consolidated Standards of Reporting Trials (CONSORT guidance) layout when reporting on a randomized controlled trial (RCT).

Read this article and then the critique.

CHANGE YOUR LIFESTYLE, SAVE YOUR LIFE?
by Francis S. Collins, M.D., Ph.D.
Director, National Institutes of Health

Like many Americans, I used to eat too much and exercise too little. I couldn't resist a plate of fresh baked goodies, and had lots of excuses about why there was never time to work out. But two years ago, I found both willpower and time upon learning that I was at risk for diabetes.

Diabetes is not something you want to get: It is a leading cause of heart attack, stroke, kidney failure, lower-limb amputations, and blindness. Nearly 2 million Americans over the age of 20 are diagnosed with diabetes each year, and that number is rising steadily. Sadly, many could have avoided or delayed getting the most common form of the disease, type 2 diabetes, by simply changing their lifestyles.

One major risk factor for diabetes is a family history of the disease. But you can still be at risk even if diabetes doesn't run in your family. In the spring of 2009, shortly before I became director of the National Institutes of Health (NIH), I had my DNA scanned to look for hereditary risks of disease. I was familiar with the scanning technologies because they arose from the Human Genome Project, the effort I previously led to read out the 3 billion letters in the human DNA instruction book. But I wasn't expecting the scans to reveal that I had two copies of a specific genetic variant associated with increased risk of type 2 diabetes. My own lab is involved in the search for diabetes genes, so this was sobering news. It looked like diabetes might be in my future unless I changed my ways.

To determine what actions to take, I turned to science. When many people think of NIH—the nation's biomedical research agency—they picture researchers in high-tech labs exploring new ways to detect and treat disease. NIH does indeed do that. But we also support studies that look at how diet, exercise, and other lifestyle factors may *prevent* disease and promote wellness.

The strategy that caught my attention came from the NIH-funded Diabetes Prevention Program trial, which found the combination of increased physical activity and modest weight loss is a highly effective way to lower risk of type-2 diabetes. Trial participants all had pre-diabetes, which is an elevation of glucose in the blood. But when they exercised 2 ½ hours a week and lost 7 % of their weight on average, many were protected from developing diabetes, with the preventive benefits lasting at least a decade. Now United Health Group is working with Walgreens and the YMCA to put these findings into practice in the real world by offering exercise and healthy eating programs in 13 communities across the nation.

While I hadn't yet developed signs of pre-diabetes, the principles of diabetes prevention were firmly laid down by this NIH study. So, I decided to adopt that same approach. Out went my indulgences of honey buns, giant muffins, venti lattes, and other sweet treats. In came small, frequent snacks of almonds, yogurt, and other high-protein, nutritious foods. I also stepped up my physical activity, hiring a personal trainer and committing myself to working out three times a week. In the first six months of my new routine, I lost 25 pounds, about 12% of my weight. I've kept that off ever since. My percentage of body fat went from 24% to 14%, and I can chest press 135 pounds. I've never felt more fit.

But we need many more happy endings. Right now, more than one-third of U.S. adults have blood sugar levels indicating they're at serious risk of developing diabetes. If you're a bit overweight, ask your doctor if you should get a glucose tolerance test to find out if you're one of them. Even if you're not, taking charge of your health by choosing the right foods and the right exercise program is among the most important investments you can makes in your future. America, it's time to change your lifestyle – it just might save your life.

http://www.nih.gov/about/director/articles.htm

Critique by Audrey Zenner

Francis S. Collins, M.D., Ph.D. offers valuable information from his own personal experiences in Change Your Lifestyle, Save Your Life? Faced with the prospect of diabetes, he decided to change his eating habits and exercise routine. Currently, this is a tremendous problem in the United States, and Americans must pay attention to change this pattern. "Nearly 2 million Americans over the age of 20 are diagnosed with diabetes each year, and that number is rising steadily. Sadly, many could have avoided or delayed getting the most common form of the disease, type 2 diabetes, by simply changing their lifestyles." In this short, but practical article, Collins educates the readers about how one may be predisposed to diabetes through their family history.

Specifically, the author cited a diabetes trial; wherein, the pre-diabetic participants were regimented to a healthier diet, increased exercise and additional lifestyle changes. For those active participants, they lost a nice percentage of weight, recouped energy, and extended protection from developing full-blown diabetes for ten years or longer. Personally, I have had to watch my diet and exercise my entire life since I can gain weight very easily. I can attest to a better feeling overall when trim and fit. Optimistically, real time programs similar to this trial are on the horizon.

The author's claims are well founded since over one-third of American adults are at the brink of pre-diabetes with elevated blood sugar levels. This timely information should be taken very seriously since the young adults of today are raising up children with bad eating habits and worse "couch potato" lifestyles. Dr. Collins has presented a noteworthy article here, and we should all follow his lead.

As you can see, my first line mentions the author's name and title of the article. The target audience is overweight Americans, or just about anyone who has gained weight. I have quoted directly from the article to support current diabetes' statistics. In the second paragraph, I briefly describe a diabetes clinical trial along with my own personal relation to the topic and agreement on how to control weight. Finally, my concluding paragraph further clarifies how this text may be woven into our lifestyles to live a long and healthy life.

Remember, when writing your own critiques:

- Firstly, give explanation as to the author's ideas. Incorporate some of the specific sentences supporting the given viewpoints.
- Propose your own opinions on the arguments while detailing points of agreement and disagreement.
- Summarize, quote, or paraphrase specific textual excerpts providing evidence for your opinions.
- Clarify how this text supports your opinions.

Critique this article using the background information on page 244:

National Institutes of Health (NIH), Essays on Science and Society
GENOME-SEQUENCING ANNIVERSARY
Faces of the Genome

Francis S. Collins, *Director, Nat'l Institutes of Health, Bethesda, MD, USA.*

When the draft sequence of the human genome* was published in February 2001, *Nature* and *Science* featured human faces on their covers. As striking as these images were, they could be seen as more art than science, because systematic genome-wide sequencing had yet to be applied to individuals for medical purposes. What a difference a decade makes. Real faces are now appearing that demonstrate the medical value of comprehensive genome sequencing.

Researchers with NIH's Undiagnosed Diseases Program recently identified a genetic cause for a rare and debilitating vascular disorder that had baffled the medical field and evaded diagnosis. The discovery was spurred by the cases of Louise Benge and Paula Allen, two middle-aged sisters from Kentucky who had calcification of the large blood vessels and joints in their hands and feet, in the absence of any effect on coronary arteries. Thanks to genomic analyses (just published in the *New England Journal of Medicine*), they now know that their severe leg and joint pain stems from a mutation in *NT5E*, which encodes a protein that converts AMP to adenosine. Better understanding of the disease mechanism will help to guide development of treatments for such patients, as well as illuminate metabolic pathways involved in calcification.

An even more impressive story of the revolution that genomic analysis is bringing to the clinic relates to Nic Volker (shown above), a 6-year-old Wisconsin boy who developed inflammatory bowel disease shortly before his second birthday. Multiple intestinal fistulas occurred, making it impossible for him to eat normally. Despite numerous tests and more than 100 surgeries, doctors remained at loss for a diagnosis and the little boy grew sicker. Then, researchers at the Medical College of Wisconsin carried out whole-exome sequencing, examining the protein-coding regions of every gene in Nic's genome. They identified a mutation in his *XIAP* gene. *XIAP* mutations were not previously associated with bowel symptoms, but had been linked to a severe blood disorder that is curable through bone marrow transplantation. The medical team raised the possibility of a transplant, which would not have been considered without a firm diagnosis. It was performed in July 2010, using stem cells from the cord blood of a matched, healthy donor. Seven months later, Nic appears to be on the road to recovery. While he is still on immunosuppressants, doctors report the new stem cells are stably engrafted, blood counts are good, and there's been no return of bowel disease. More important to Nic, he can finally eat solid foods!

http://journals.lww.com/geneticsinmedicine/Documents/GIM200819_Revised.pdf

The Human Genome Project – Background Information

Begun formally in 1990, the U.S. Human Genome Project was a 13-year effort coordinated by the U.S. Department of Energy and the National Institutes of Health. The project originally was planned to last 15 years, but rapid technological advances accelerated the completion date to 2003. Project goals:

- identify all the approximately 20,000-25,000 genes in human DNA,
- determine the sequences of the 3 billion chemical base pairs that make up human DNA,
- store this information in databases,
- improve tools for data analysis,
- transfer related technologies to the private sector, and
- address the ethical, legal, and social issues (ELSI) that may arise from the project.

To help achieve these goals, researchers also studied the genetic makeup of several nonhuman organisms. These include the common human gut bacterium Escherichia coli, the fruit fly, and the laboratory mouse.

A unique aspect of the U.S. Human Genome Project is that it was the first large scientific undertaking to address potential ELSI implications arising from project data.

Another important feature of the project was the federal government's long-standing dedication to the transfer of technology to the private sector. By licensing technologies to private companies and awarding grants for innovative research, the project catalyzed the multibillion-dollar U.S. biotechnology industry and fostered the development of new medical applications.

Landmark papers detailing sequence and analysis of the human genome were published in February 2001 and April 2003 issues of Nature and Science. See an index of these papers and learn more about the insights gained from them.

http://www.ornl.gov/sci/techresources/Human_Genome/project/about.shtml

Practice Writing

Now, it's time to begin writing your critique. Write in standard essay form, beginning with the introduction identifying the subject and your personal opinion. Be sure to defend your views by highlighting detailed concerns toward the arguments. Your conclusion will reiterate your argument along with restating your opinions.

Exercise 10-B

Consider the following questions before writing:

1. Are the arguments reasonable?
2. Does the author present correct facts?
3. Are important terms well defined?
4. Is there enough evidence to substantiate the arguments?
5. Is the writing suitable for the proposed audience?
6. Are pros and cons offered?
7. Does the text improve your understanding of the subject?
8. Are there any areas that stimulate a significant response from you? If so, make note of them and your specific reaction.
9. Think back on how you have been influenced by the topic. Has this writing swayed you one way or the other?
10. What queries and/or opinions does this text bring to mind?

WRITE YOUR CRITIQUE HERE

SECTION 11

Curriculum Vitae

&

Resumes

CREATING CURRICULUM VITAE

A curriculum vita (CV) is similar to a resume, yet exclusively used in the academic field summarizing your academic educational background. The main objective of the CV is to present your credentials for a position in the academic field of employment. This may be geared towards a fellowship, grant, and/or academic position in an educational institution. The average length of the CV runs from 2-4 pages, but senior scholars quite often produce several more pages of content. Since each discipline maintains their own standards, become knowledgeable as to your own discipline's requirements. The main objective of your CV is to offer a clear synopsis of your education in an efficiently well-ordered communication that will prompt the search committee to offer you an interview.

The following papers are usually required when making application for an academic position:

- Curriculum Vitae

- Dissertation Abstract

- Statement of Research Interests

- Statement of Teaching Interests

Essential materials to include with your CV:

Completed application

Education information

Dissertation title & author
scholarly interests

Awards/honors/patents
interests

Grants/fellowships/scholarships

Research experience

Teaching experience

Publications & presentations

Related professional experiences

Languages

Memberships in associations, organizations, societies, clubs

Recommendation letters

Cover letter

Abstract of dissertation

Statement of research &

Statement of teaching

Course list

Curriculum Vitae

Each and every page of your CV should include your name at the top of the page. Your full name, address, phone number, fax number, and email address should appear on page number one. Page numbers are necessary on every page except the first page. Remember to use a professional email address and voice mail.

Education

Beginning with the most recent university attended, list your degrees in reverse order. Be sure to type in the institution's name and date you received your degree. If you have not yet graduated from your degree program, type in the expected date of graduation with the degree to be awarded. Additionally, names of advisors with thesis and/or dissertation titles are deemed necessary.

Honors & Awards (Grants, Fellowships, Scholarships, Patents, Copyrights, etc.)

If you have numerous items to report, place them towards the beginning of your CV. Otherwise, if you have few, you may mention them later in the CV. Your strengths should be highlighted toward the beginning of the CV. Also, research-linked and dissertation-supported accolades should be cited near the beginning of your CV. If you have accrued several research grants, do not hesitate to create a separate section for this.

Research Experience

Researchers ought to supply information on postdoctoral, doctoral, graduate, and undergraduate research. Briefly and concisely describe the projects with their names, list institution names, professors, and dates. Explain what contribution you made to the project. (Appending "Statement of Research Interests" is acceptable.)

Teaching Experience

The "Statement of Teaching Interests" is required for teaching positions. Describe what you are proficient to teach. When responding to a teaching position, be sure and make note in your cover letter that you are fully capable of teaching such a course. What's more, list the courses you have taught, comprised of: where, what, when, and include your title when you taught the course.

Publications & Presentations

Depending upon the strength of your publication history, this section may be placed at the beginning, middle, or end of your CV. Also, you may subdivide this topic into a publication's section using standard bibliographic forms (you may break this down to Books, Abstracts, Reviews, and Other Publications). If you have several Papers and Presentations, you may want to include dates and locations with titles. Published abstracts should be listed as a separate section.

Professional Experience

This section can glorify your experiences in professional associations, committees, teaching, research, tutoring, and administration.

Languages

Native, fluent, read only

Study or travel abroad

International studies, foreign travel

Technical and Specialized Skills

Computer skills, etc.

Related/Other Experience

Other related work experience

References

At the end of the CV, list three references that you will notify and supply them with a copy of your CV. Include their formal title, name, institution, address, telephone, email, and fax.

Cover Letter

Compose a one page cover letter that concisely states why you are interested in applying for the position and your pertinent background. Direct them to your attached curriculum vitae for additional information on your attributes. Never discuss any of the CV material in this cover letter. If possible, type the letter on your department's letter head paper with your professional address.

Dissertation Abstract

This should be appended at the end of the CV.

Statement of Research & Scholarly Interests
This 2-4 page accounting explains all of your research interests (past, current, and future). Keep in mind, to detail past and present research methodologies, lab skills, plus end results. Your future section should entail the next 3-5 years and describe your plans, including undergraduate, graduate, and post-doc students involved in your research. Most often, the impetus for this work dates back to your postdoctoral studies.

Ready to Begin Preparing Your CV   Vita = singular Vitae = plural

Typical vita categories or headings may include some or all of the following:

Personal/Contact Information
--name
--address
--phone number(s)
--email
--profile link

Academic Background
--postgraduate work
--graduate work/degree(s), major/minors, thesis/dissertation titles, honors
--undergraduate degree(s), majors/minors, honors

Professional Licenses/Certifications
Academic/Teaching Experience
--courses taught, courses introduced
--innovation in teaching
--teaching evaluations

Technical and Specialized Skills
Related/Other Experience
--other work experience

Professional/Academic Honors and Awards
Professional development
--conferences/workshops attended, other activities

Research/Scholarly Activities
--journal articles
--conference proceedings
--books
--chapters in books
--magazine articles
--papers presented/workshops
--work currently under submission
--work in progress

Grants
Service
--academic
--professional
--community

Academic/Research Interests
Affiliations/memberships
Foreign language abilities/skills
Consulting
Volunteer work
References
Other CV-related resources that can help: your choice

SAMPLE CV

Jane Doe
211 Evergreen Court
Carmel City, CA 90000
111.000.1111
jdoe@email.com

EDUCATION San Francisco Graduate School of Psychology *San Francisco, California,*

Ph.D. Candidate, Clinical Psychology	**June 2009**

Emphasis: Clinical, Development Psychology
Recipient: Israeli Student Scholarship (Academic)
San Francisco State University *San Francisco, California*

M.A., Developmental Psychology	**June 2003**

Thesis: Self-esteem, Parenting Styles, Communication:
Determining a Developmental Link
Emphasis: Counseling Electives, Practicum
San Francisco State University, *San Francisco, California*

B.A., Psychology	**June 2000**

San Francisco State University, *San Francisco, California*

PRACTICA Counselor (designate)
San Francisco Child Study, *San Francisco, California*
Observed/assisted with individual children and adolescent
therapy (testing, diagnosis, and care presentation). **11/1999 – 7/2001**

Counselor H.E.L.P Line, *San Francisco, California*
Telephone counselor for 24- hour child abuse hotline. Provided
crisis intervention, education, and counseling to parents.
Maintained knowledge of related referral network. **12/2002 – 6/2003**

Intern Private Practice of Richard J. Damp, Ph.D., *Carmel, California*
Obtained psycho-medical histories, observed therapy
sessions, discussed treatment **3/1999 – 7/1999**

RESEARCH

Research Assistant
San Francisco Psychological Services *San Francisco, California*
Assisted Dr. Richard Servatti with an anxiety research project.
Served as an actor-facilitator, creating anxiety-response
behaviors in subjects during videotaped session.

8/1998 –2/1999

Researcher Anonymous School, University of California
Supervised by the Dean of Social Sciences for U.C., Irvine.
Conducted pre- and post-class testing and follow-up. *Irvine, CA* **4/1997 – 7/1998**

TEACHING

Teaching Assistant
Anonymous School, *San Francisco, California*
Taught students 12-15 years of age, library and study skills unit.
Provided one on one and group psycho-educational counseling. **7/2001 – Present**

AFFILIATIONS American Psychological Association (APA)
California Psychological Association (CPA)

FOREIGN LANGUAGE
Spanish (fluent: speak, write, read, and translate)

Strong Action Verbs to Embellish a Resume/CV

By using simple expressions conveyed with passive verbs, you are not presenting yourself in the best light. Begin thinking in terms of more action with strength that communicates a more vivid interpretation of why the employer should hire you. Your true value must portray how you will benefit the employer. In this day and age, with so many people looking for work, your resume or CV must be stellar; enthrall that employer to sit up and focus on you.

abated	*diverted*	*interpreted*
abbreviated	*doubled*	*leveraged*
accelerated	*enforced*	*masterminded*
authored	*enhanced*	*maximized*
benefited	*enthralled*	*mentored*
branded	*exceeded*	*optimized*
broached	*focused*	*orchestrated*
captivated	*forged*	*pioneered*
captured	*formalized*	*proliferated*
championed	*formulated*	*progressed*
consolidated	*generated*	*recaptured*
conveyed	*influenced*	*re-engineered*
critiqued	*initiated*	*rejuvenated*
directed	*integrated*	*spearheaded*
diversified	*intensified*	*structured*

The point here is to put action verbs into your resume or CV that strongly communicate how you approach each job as action oriented with targeted results to benefit the employer!

SAMPLE CV

John Smith
Street, City, State, Zip
Phone: 555-555-5555
Cell: 555-666-6666
email@email.com

Objective: Assistant Professor, Psychology

Education:
Ph.D., Psychology, University of Minnesota, Minneapolis, MN   2006
Concentrations: Psychology, Community Psychology
Dissertation: A Study of ESL Learning Disabled Children

M.A., Psychology, University at Albany, New York   2003
Concentrations: Psychology, Special Education
Thesis: Communication Skills of Learning Disabled Children

B.A, Psychology, California State University, Long Beach, CA   2000

Experience:
Instructor   2004 - 2006
University of Minnesota
Course: Psychology in the Classroom

Teaching Assistant   2002 - 2003
University at Albany
Courses: Special Education, Learning Disabilities

Research Skills:
Extensive knowledge of SPSSX and SAS statistical programs.

Presentations:
Smith John (2006). The behavior of ESL learning disabled children in the classroom. Paper presented at the Psychology Conference at the University of Minnesota, Minneapolis, MN.

Publications:

Smith, John (2005). The behavior of ESL learning disabled children in the classroom. Journal of ESL Educational Psychology, 19 - 24.

Grants and Fellowships:
- RDB Grant (University of Minnesota Research Grant, 2005), $2,000
- Workshop Grant (for ESL meeting in New York, 2004), $1,500

Awards and Honors:
- Treldar Scholar   2005
- Academic Excellent Award   2003

Skills and Qualifications:
- Microsoft Office, Internet
- Programming ability in C++ and PHP
- Fluent in German, French and Spanish

References:

Excellent references available upon request.

Stuart W. Monroe
1234 Central Avenue
Anytown, ST, USA, XXXXX
telephone: 1-XXX-XXX-XXXX
e-mail: XXXX@xxx.net

EDUCATION

Graduate College of the University of Educators, NY, NY
Ph.D. American History   **2001**
Dissertation: "America the Beautiful Early Days in the
Nineteenth Century"
Advisor: Dr. E.W. Ewing

State University, NY, NY
M.A., American History   **1987**

State University, NY, NY
B.A., Secondary Education in History, English minor   **1980**

TEACHING EXPERIENCE

State University of Illinois, Chicago, IL   **2010 – present**
Lecturer, American History

City Colleges of Chicago, Chicago, IL   **2001 - 2010**
Taught junior college, U.S. history

Chicago Public Schools, Chicago, IL   **2001 - 2010**
Taught high school U.S. history

PROFESSIONAL AFFILIATIONS

Illinois Association of Historical Studies

American Historical Association

Western History Association

Organization of American Higher Education

PUBLICATIONS

Books

American History Revisited, 1850-1900. Paperback edition, Chicago: Printers' Publishers, 2000.

The Civil War from the North's Point of View (contributing editor). Chicago: Reader's Books, 1998.

Little Bighorn, March-September 1876. Chicago: Printers' Publishers, 1993.

Buffalo Bill: A Guide to History & the Western Film. Chicago: State University Press and Readers' Books, 1990.

Articles

Monroe, S.W. (winter 2005). Hand Combat. State Journal of Military History, 61-75.

Monroe, S.W. (2003). Historical Battlefields. National Journal of American History, 31-42.

Monroe, S.W. (September 2002). Toward A Last Stand: History or Myth? *15th Annual Custer Symposium Proceedings,* 22-33.

Book Reviews

Review of **American Warriors**, by H. J. Veronico. *The American Observer*, April 1994.

Review of **The Oregon Trail,** by Francis Pullman. *The American Observer*, December 1992.

Review of **High Noon: Violence on the Western Frontier**, John M. Collins. *The American Scholar,* March 1989.

Style Advice for CVs

Gapping

Gapping is the deletion of certain words. This is preferred in a CV since you want to express your message using the least amount of words necessary. The elements that are generally deleted are: first person pronouns, auxiliary verbs, articles, relative clause elements and some prepositional phrases.

I am fluent in Mandarin Chinese.	vs.	*Fluent in Mandarin Chinese*

I am a native-speaker of Mandarin, and I have an advanced knowledge of Japanese and English.	vs.	<u>*Languages*</u> *Mandarin native* *Japanese superior* *English high advanced*

The grants that I have received are the X, Y, and Z grants.	vs.	<u>*Grants received*</u> *X Grant* *Y Grant* *Z Grant*

Action-orientation

Try to make your CV as action-oriented as possible. Using verbs (often, but not always) puts more focus on your achievements rather than just your status or job.

Instructor for advanced-level calculus	vs.	*Taught advanced-level calculus*

Chaperone for study abroad on excursion to Germany	vs.	*Accompanied students on study abroad to Germany*

Lab equipment maintenance person	vs.	*Maintained lab equipment*

Sometimes the participial verb comes first (e.g, *accompanied students*....).
Other times, the participial verb comes after the noun. Look at these examples.

Languages spoken: French, Spanish, Italian

Courses taught: Introduction to Western Civilization, American
                      History from 1607 to 1775

Grants received: 2000-2001, Rivera Grant ($12,000) for archival
                      research on Piedmont Bluegrass in the early 20th century

Full forms of these reduced participles would be: *The languages that I speak...*

The courses that I have taught...

The grants that I have received...

Consistent parallels

Keep in mind that you are striving for ease of reading for your audience.
Therefore, try to keep most everything consistently parallel. Especially, verb
forms throughout the CV should follow the same patterns in tense and form.
That way your reader can easily skim and/or scan your credentials.

Read the following CV with a discriminating eye. Then, answer the subsequent questions.

Janet Doe
101 Main Street
New York, NY 11379
Phone: 555-555-5555
Cell: 555-666-6666
Email: email@email.com

PROFESSIONAL EXPERIENCE

Consulting Physician	*2005 - Present*
Private Practice	
New York, NY	

Attending Physician	*1995 – 2005*
New York Public Hospital	
New York, NY	

Associate Professor	*1998 - Present*
Department of Psychiatry	
New York Public Hospital	
New York, NY	

Assistant Professor	*1990 - 1998*
Department of Psychiatry	
New York Public Hospital	
New York, NY	

EDUCATION

New York Medical School   **1982**
MD
New York, NY

Rochester Medical School   **1974**
MS
Rochester, NY

Clintonville College   **1972**
BS
Hastings, NY

BOARD CERTIFICATION

- National Board of Psychiatric Medicine

MEDICAL LICENSURE

- New York State License

GRADUATE TRAINING

Fellowship   **1986-1988**
Neurology and Neurophysiology
Florida, Hospital
Tampa, FL

Residency   **1983-1986**
Neuropsychiatry
Dallas Hospital, Dallas, TX

Internship   **1982-1983**
Psychiatry
New York Hospital, New York, NY

PUBLICATIONS

Preventing Drug Abuse (2008)

APA (American Publication Association), New York, NY

Family Medical Interventions (2005)

APA (American Publication Association), New York, NY

MEMBERSHIPS AND ASSOCIATIONS

- A.M.A,
- U.S.P.A. Psychiatric Association
- US Assoc. of Women in Psychiatry

Exercise 11-A

CV Comments

Format

Is it easy to read? Is it easy to see what has been accomplished? Is there anything you would change?

Missing information

Is there anything you would add? Are there any questions you have that the CV should answer?

Deletions

Is there anything you would leave out? Is there anything that just takes up valuable space?

English

Do you notice any English mistakes?

Exercise 11-B

Curriculum Vitae (T/F)

The expression *curriculum vita* is Latin for "course of life". It is a description of your education and your career. In American English, it is often referred to as a *CV* while in British English you may see it written as *c.v.*

Look at the following statements and see if you agree with them or not?

1. A résumé and CV are exactly the same thing? (Please make sure you know how to pronounce *résumé*.)

2. You should include your birth date, gender, nationality, and marital status.

3. Your CV should include both your home and departmental addresses.

4. It is best to use reverse chronological order. (Put more recent items first.)

5. The longer your CV is, the better it is.

6. Under the section for current education, you should put the working title of your dissertation, abstract and the name of your advisor.

7. Provide some information about your high school education.

8. List computer skills and expertise in using special equipment.

9. List all languages you know and how well you know them.

10. List published articles.

11. The type font for your name at the top of your CV should be bold and larger than the rest of the text in your CV.

12. Provide references at the end of your CV even if you have included them in your application letter.

Template, Sample Academic Curriculum Vita

Name
Address
City, State, Zip
Telephone, Cell Phone
Email
Online Profile

SUMMARY STATEMENT (Optional) Include a brief explanation/list of the highlights of your candidacy.

EDUCATION
List your academic background, including undergraduate and graduate institutions attended.

Graduate Institution, City, State, Country Degree, Major Dissertation	**Date**
Graduate Institution, City, State, Country Degree, Major Dissertation	**Date**
Undergraduate Institution, City, State Degree, Major	**Date**

EMPLOYMENT HISTORY
List in reverse chronological order, include position details.   **Dates**

POSTDOCTORAL TRAINING
List your postdoctoral experiences, if applicable.   **Dates**

FELLOWSHIPS
List internships/fellowships, including organization & your title   **Dates**

LICENSES / CERTIFICATION
List type of license, certification or accreditation received.   **Dates**

PUBLICATIONS / BOOKS
PROFESSIONAL AFFILIATIONS
SKILLS / INTERESTS

SAMPLE RESUME, International

Maria Cristina Rosa
Santa Maria S. 212 Villa
Santiago, Chile, South America
Phone: 1-111-1111
E-mail: abc@xyz.com
Online profile

Objective: An entry-level position with opportunity to utilize valuable liberal arts education, TEFL Certificate, and Spanish conversational skills

Education

University of California-Irvine with Universidad de Andrès Bello	**8/2005 – 12/2005**

TEFL Certificate (Teaching English as a Foreign Language) Santiago, Chile

University of Minnesota, Morris, MN	**2002**

B.A. Sociology, 3.8 G.P.A

English Language Teaching Assistant Program	**2002**

Chile, South America

Awards Received: Dean's List, Junior/ Senior, University of Minnesota, Freshman Academic Scholarship, National Honor Society

Interests and Activities: Gymnastics, Students Against Destructive Decisions, Vice-President, Treasurer, Converse in Spanish, teach English to Spanish-speakers
Languages: English, Spanish

Work Experience

Colegio Umbral de Curauma Valparaiso, Chile, South America	**2006 - present**

English as Foreign Language Teacher's Assistant

Private English as Foreign Language Teacher, Valparaiso, Chile	**2006 - present**

CEIAT Centro Educacion Intregada de Adultos Talagante,
Talagante, Chile, South America

English as Foreign Language Teacher -Substitute/Volunteer	**2006**

Sarah Smith

CAMPUS:
789 Lincoln Hall
Normal, IL 67890
111-222-3333
ssmith@ilstu.edu

PERMANENT:
123 Main Street
Anytown, CA 12345
777-888-9999
ssmith@gmail.com

OBJECTIVE: Auditor position, public accounting, Chicago area.

SUMMARY:
- Advanced accounting, auditing experience
- Auditor internship, Ernst & Young, New York
- BBA, accounting, graduated with high honors
- MS Office, Windows XP, Internet.

EDUCATION: **Bachelor's of Business Administration, Accounting   5/2008**
Illinois State University, Normal, Illinois
(Graduated w/High Honors)

EXPERIENCE: **Auditor Internship   5/2007 – 8/2007**
Ernst & Young, New York, New York
Contributed to annual audit, ABC Holdings
Assisted with quarterly audit of Home Town Bank
Developed Excel spreadsheet macros decreasing entry time, automatically cross-referencing errors
Received Employee of the Month award —first intern to win award

Accounts Payable/Bookkeeping Clerk   5/2005 - Present
Pleasantville, Tax & Bookkeeping Service
Pleasantville, New York
Assisted (via remote) with payroll, tax, account processing
Developed automated monthly sales tax payment system
Implemented Rapid Tax Refund service for individual customers.

ACTIVITIES:
Vice President, Student Accounting	**2007-2008**
Treasurer, Illinois State Student Government	**2007-2008**
Dorm Resident Assistant	**2006-2008**

Sample Resume Template

NAME
Address Line 1   Phone
City, State/Province Postal Code   e-mail, online
online profile

Objective: Type 1-3 lines briefly stating your goals.

Qualifications

Using action words to maximize the impact, describe how your background and
strengths would make you a strong candidate for the position you are seeking.
This section should be concise, contain action words, and should sell your most
marketable experiences and abilities.

Education

Degree-BA obtained, field of study, school name & location   **Graduation Date**
Degree-MA obtained, field of study, school name & location   **Graduation Date**

Employment

Position, Name of Company, City, State, Country   **Dates**
In the same manner as above, describe your first job
responsibilities. Be concise; remove all unnecessary words
and phrases. Include specific results of your actions or
decisions to demonstrate your contribution.

Position, Name of Company, City, State, Country   **Dates**
In the same manner as above, describe your next (or current) job.

Position, Name of Company, City, State, Country   **Dates**
In the same manner as above, describe your next (or current) job.

Position, Name of Company, City, State, Country   **Dates**
In the same manner as above, describe your current or most recent job.

Awards
Professional Affiliations
Computer Skills
Excellent referrals supplied upon request

(Use footers with pages numbers, name, season, year)

Digital Resumes & CVs

Resumes and CVs are surfacing on the Internet, and I suggest that you join in. Let your imagination create a marketable online version. Employers appreciate this method of promoting yourself, and it gives you credibility as someone who is keeping up with technology and has valuable computer skills. The convenience of this resume/CV format allows for speedier transmission of your information and online networking. This form of communication may hyperlink or embed to a video, social-media or online portfolio. If you would like an easy method of posting your profile online, just go to the LinkedIn website, follow the instructions for their resume builder, and customize your text to fit. As a matter of fact, this website will also supply you with a link to share your resume or CV with others. Additionally, there are many other free online resume builders that will enable you to do the same. For those of you, who already have your own website, consider posting it there. When positioned in academia, one may opt for use of a "home page" that serves as a site for professors to share their profiles with others. Here, you may present your resume/CV in its entirety or simply give a link to your full resume/CV. Do not forget to include key words the employer may be looking for; of course, you may have no idea what that might be. For that reason, look at vocabulary in the job advertisement to give yourself an educated guess. Also, job titles you have held, skills you have acquired, and software you are acquainted with all make fine examples of key words. If and when you have trouble thinking of keywords, go ahead and research journals and websites in your field of study for the specific vocabulary. After completing the file, save it using words that are pertinent to your job search; for example, labresearcher, IT, geriatricnursing, or civilengineer. If you use any wording; such as, jim'sresume or mycurriculumvita, it may not reach the decision-maker's desk; in this day and age, so many resumes are being sent that you need any advantage possible.

SECTION 12

Cover Letters
&
E-Mail

Cover Letter and Resume Customization

Each cover letter you send along with your CV or resume should be customized for the recipient employer. Accordingly, the generic parts of your letter may be repeated, but every letter must be tailored to each job and employer.

Recipient Employer: To which employer will you be submitting your resume and cover letter?

Specific Named Individual:

Cover letters should be addressed to the specific name of the decision maker. Quite frequently, obstacles will obstruct finding the name of the particular hiring manager; nonetheless, persist. You may phone the business and ask who the hiring manager is for a certain position. Also, an Internet search may prove resourceful. If luck does not succeed, begin your letter with "Dear Hiring Manager for _____{position name}."

Specific Position: What precise job are you targeting with your resume and cover letter?

Do not list numerous possible positions or say that you're willing to consider any position. If you do, the employer will see you as unfocused or even desperate.

Explicit Qualifications/Requirements: List the explicit qualifications for the job position you are applying for. If you're responding to a want ad/Internet job posting, you should find qualifications given in it. When making a cold-contact with the employer, you may need to investigate the qualifications.

Definite Examples: List definite examples of how you fulfill the job requirements.

Detailed benefits to employer: Detail very specifically how you will meet the employer's needs, resolve the employer's problems; otherwise, benefit the hiring company.

Sample Cover Letter

January 1, 20XX

Ms. Janet Jones
President
J.J. Accounting Inc.
123 S. State Street
Chicago, IL 12345

Ms. Jones:

Mr. James Colwell, a partner with your New York office, referred me to you. He informed me that your Chicago office is aggressively seeking quality trainees for your auditor development program.

I have accounting experience for more than two years, including as an auditor intern last year with the New York City office of Ernst & Young. I will be receiving my Bachelors of Arts Degree with high honors this May from Illinois State University. I am assured that my practical work experience and concrete educational experience has prepared me well for making an immediate contribution to J.J. Accounting. I understand the level of professionalism and communication required for long-standing success in this field. I plan on being a motivated auditor upon completion of your development program.

I will be in the Chicago area the week of January 23. I will contact your office to inquire as to a potential meeting date and time. I look forward to meeting you then.

Sincerely,

Kimberlee Kraft
789 Lincoln Hall
Normal, IL 67890
217-222-3456
e-mail

This type of cover letter will pay back far greater returns than the simple introduction to me letter that most people use. Remember that a successful cover letter is a marketing tool used to move your customer one step closer to buying your product. Customers do not buy features, they buy benefits. So make sure you drive home your benefit to the customer!

Your cover letter should always be personalized. To whom it may concern is an immediate turnoff.

Keep in mind that many employers look to the cover letter as an example of your written communication skills. Resumes are often written and proofread by others, but cover letters are typically never proofed. Make certain your cover letter is spell-checked, grammar-checked, and proofread by someone other than yourself.

I realize that no matter how many times or ways I say it, people will copy this example cover letter almost verbatim. If you do, you will be spotted as having used a canned letter. Take the time to do it right.

Cover Letter Components Worksheet

The opening of your cover letter should wow the reader with impact to urge him/her to continue reading. This worksheet will assist you in providing just that; yet, it is mandatory for each letter to be written uniquely and precisely for you. That is, not one that any applicant could have written to any employer. Be brief in your cover letter. In no way, never type more than one page and stay under a full page. Each paragraph should have about three sentences.

Exercise 12-A

First Paragraph

Without wasting any time, the first paragraph must spark the employer's interest, offer information on the benefits you can bring to the company, while making you shine above all other job-seekers. Focus on three benefits you can offer the employer.

Weak opening paragraph: I am writing today to apply for the research manager position you have posted on your company website.

Better opening paragraph: I have increased the size and research levels of my laboratories in every position I have held, which in turn has increased the revenues and profits of my employers. I want to contribute this same success in the research manager position you have posted on your website.

Below, develop a draft first paragraph for your own cover letter, telling why you're writing, what position you're targeting, and emphasizing your unique proposition:

_____

_____

_____

_____

Exercise 12-B   Second Paragraph

Provide more detail about your professional and/or academic qualifications. Detail more information about how you can contribute the benefits you mention in the first paragraph. Be sure to stress accomplishments and achievements rather than job duties and responsibilities. If you're responding to a job posting or ad, be sure to tailor this paragraph to the employer needs described in the advertisement.

Also, show what you know about the employer. Relate yourself to the organization, giving details why you should be considered for the position. Research the employer – demonstrate that you know something about the organization.

Below, develop a draft 2nd paragraph expanding on how you can contribute to the employer's success, especially in relation to the employer's needs (usually stated in the ad/job posting):

_____

_____

_____

_____

_____

_____

_____

_____

_____

_____

Exercise 12-C   Third Paragraph

The final paragraph of your cover letter must be proactive – and request action. Ask for the job interview (or a meeting) in this paragraph. Express your confidence that you are a perfect fit for the position. Put the employer on notice that you plan to follow up within a specified time.

Weak closing paragraph: I hope you will review my resume, and if you agree with what I have stated here, consider me for the position. I look forward to hearing from you soon.

Better closing paragraph: I am eager to help advance your company's success and convinced that we should arrange a meeting time. In the next week, I will call your office to schedule an appointment.

Below, develop a draft 3rd paragraph reinforcing your fit for the job, requesting an interview, and telling the employer how you plan to follow up:

_____

_____

_____

_____

_____

_____

_____

_____

_____

_____

<u>E-Mail</u> **Sample Letter Version** — *Typed directly onto opening page of e-mail message.*

Subject: *(logical to recipient!)* Application for research job

January dd, yyyy

Mr. A.H. Higgins
Director, Human Resources
XYZ Chemical Company
2747 David Avenue
Roselle, IL 60172
ahhiggins@xyzchemical.com

Dear Mr. Higgins:

I am interested in applying for the research job advertised on your company's website, posted 12/11/2012. Along with my research background, training, and work experience, I believe I would make a valuable contribution to the XYZ Chemical Company.

Both internships and graduate research assistant positions have prepared me well to work in the chemical engineering field. Also, I have completed courses in statistics and research methods.

I believe my combination of education and experience is an excellent match for the research position described. Enclosed is a copy of my resume with additional information about my qualifications. Thank you very much for your consideration. I look forward to receiving your reply and making an appointment for an interview.

Sincerely,

Sam Student
000 Fork Road
Kansas City, Kansas 11111
222-333-4444
sstudent@gmail.com

Cover Letters Format

The purpose of a cover letter is TO GET YOU AN INTERVIEW.

Know something about your employer (or funder)

Explain how your goals and interests are ideally suited to the employer

Try to address the letter to a specific individual. MAKE SURE YOU SPELL THE NAME CORRECTLY.

If a blind letter:	To Whom It May Concern:
	Dear Sir/Madam:
	Dear Search Committee:

Often a cover letter is three paragraphs, but it can be more.

Paragraph 1	---	Identify yourself.
	---	Mention the position you are interested in.
	---	Mention where you saw the position advertised
	---	Indicate why you are interested in the employer, e.g. ,a specific research area.
Paragraph 2	---	Describe the skills and experiences that make you well-suited for the position.
	---	HIGHLIGHT the important information from your CV. Make sure you give more details than just the CV, about two or three specific areas. Also, do not copy verbatim from your CV.

Paragraph 3   ---   Make a request for a face-to-face meeting. e.g., I look forward to meeting you in the near future. I am looking forward to meeting with you to discuss more about your program and how my interests .....

                     ---   Indicate how you can be reached (optional).

                     ---   Thank the reader for taking the time to review your CV.

Miscellaneous

1. PROOFREAD (Have a native speaker whom you trust, check it.)

2. Follow all the general rules for formal academic writing (e.g., no contractions, try to avoid phrasal verbs, etc.)

3. Single-spaced within each paragraph and double-spaced between paragraphs.

4. Never send a CV without a cover letter.

5. Salary requirements/Visa requirements???? Most CV guides say no.

6. In America, we do not furnish employers with pictures of ourselves.

7. Display your professionalism.

    a. Keep personal information to a minimum. (Don't say that you want to work at UCSD because you can be close to the ocean and love surfing, for example.)

    b. Don't be too egocentric but don't disqualify yourself either. (Avoid saying how great you are. Focus on your skills and experience. Those   favorable personal comments should be made by your references in your letters of recommendation. Also, don't make statements like "Although I have never......." or "While I have not......")

8. In general, keep the cover letter to one page.

U.S. Mail

DON'T FORGET TO SIGN IT.

Don't fold it. It's better to send your cover letter and CV in a big envelope.

Never photocopy a cover letter.

Electronically

Put the cover letter in the body of the e-mail message (copy and paste).

Attach the CV.

Some companies electronically scan cover letters and resumes for key words. Make sure you have those key words in your resume. As of the present, I have never heard of optical scanners in academia.

Final Thought

Remember that flaws in your cover letter look like flaws in your qualifications. Everything must be perfect!

Websites with Samples

Here are some sites with example CVs and cover letters specifically tailored to academia.

University of Illinois at Chicago

http://www.uic.edu/depts/ocs/

University of Illinois at Urbana

http://www.careercenter.illinois.edu/students/cover-letter

American Statistical Association (specifically on Teaching Statistics in the Health Sciences)

http://www.bio.ri.ccf.org/ASA_TSHS/mockCV/ApplyingForJob.pdf

This site has all kinds of information about finding post doctoral positions.

http://www.postdocjobs.com/jobseekers/

Some suggested business closing salutations (formal):

Cordially,	**Sincerely yours,**
Best regards,	**Warm regards,**
Best wishes,	**With anticipation,**
Confidently yours,	**Yours respectfully,**
Kind regards,	**Yours sincerely,**
Kind wishes,	**Yours truly,**
Many thanks,	**Truly yours,**
Respectfully yours,	

E-Mail Conventions

E-mail is a very casual form of communication, but there still are some rules. This handout will deal with "etiquette" and how to respond to people you do not know well or people of higher status, instructors and advisors. Basically, it will give some tips on how to be casual yet polite. You have free reign with your personal e-mail.

Emoticons and Acronyms

It would be best if you did NOT use emoticons (icons of personal emotion, for example: a smiley face) with your professors. Acronyms (capital letters with periods standing for proper nouns) are different. Some are OK and some are not. Of course, use your own judgment. If you have a good relationship with your professor, go ahead. If you're not sure, err on the side of being conservative. Follow your professor's lead in use of formal or informal emails.

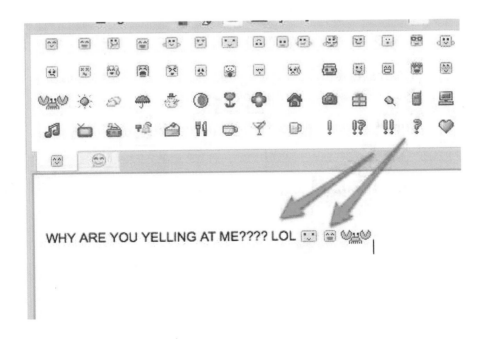

WHY ARE YOU YELLING AT ME???? LOL

Rules for Writing to Professors/Teachers

1.   Use a formal salutation, unless your teacher has specifically told you to call her/him by their first name. Address your teachers as: Dr., Professor, Mr., Mrs., or Ms. plus their family name. You do not have to use "Dear" if you feel that's too personal. Other salutations could be:

Good morning Dr. Rao:

Hello Professor Patel,

Avoid "Hey", "Hi There" or anything else too casual.

2.   Use correct spelling, punctuation, and capitalization, just use the shift key. Also, do not overuse punctuation. E-mails are not formal papers so a few mistakes may occur. Don't worry too much but don't be too informal either. E-mails with no full stops (periods) or commas are difficult to read; sometimes even changing the text meaning. Here are two inappropriate examples, please correct them.

wheres next itbe conv same plc as lst yr? r dates in feb or march? r u prsnting? i look frwrd to seeing u

soooo grateful for help w/info Thanx!!!!!!!!!!!!!!!

3.   Always write in full sentences. Too many deletions can be puzzling. Write out the full form of this message.

snd mess to members w/ convention details & cc to my mailbox asap cnt w8t

4.   DO NOT WRITE IN CAPITAL LETTERS SINCE IT SEEMS LIKE YOU ARE SHOUTING.

5.   Subject lines must be used. Again, teachers get many e-mails each day and must quickly decipher what is important to read. Try to type something that is pertinent to your email subject. Never lead your professor to believe it's spam.

6.   In replying to emails, include the original mail in your reply. Click "Reply," instead of "New Mail." If you receive many emails, obviously you cannot remember every individual email. This means by not using the previous email to simply reply to, there is not enough information resulting in much time searching for the original email. Providing this thread saves the recipient much more time and frustration in looking for the related emails in their inbox! Use "Reply to All" when there is a group of people sending you the original email.

7.   Proofread email through the recipient's viewpoint before you send it to avoid misunderstandings.

8.   In order not to annoy your recipient, do not request delivery and read receipts. His/her software might not support it, or they may have blocked it. Ask the recipient to let you know if it was received.

Common sense advice

1.   Avoid looking naive or juvenile in your email correspondence. Here are two examples that overuse many of these informal conventions.

Hi, BTW i not sure about book   in clas you sad buy it where   how much   FYI i don't have lot $ otoh book in library?

thanx soooooo much   TTYL

u can use my personal email   luvwrld@gmail.com

dear tchr,

i sorry for late to clas but i up late lasnite stdy but no more lat to clas this semester plse forgiv me

Etiquette

1.   Respond promptly. Even if you don't have an answer, reply and let your teacher know you received his/her e-mail.

2.   If you cannot respond promptly, flag the email, so you remember to attend to it later.

3.   Do not impose (require your teacher to do something for you).

4.   Give options.

5.   Make the receiver feel good.

Inappropriate E-mail:

Yo, can I make a app't about class, I don't appreciate what happened   John

Appropriate E-mail:

Dear Professor Jones:

 I'd like to meet with you sometime next week to discuss my concerns about our conversation tonight in class. I am in your Economics 777 section on Mondays and Wednesdays at 6 and am the student who missed the exam last week. I'm hoping that I might explain my absence and arrange to make up the test. May I meet with you briefly before class on Wednesday?

Email Etiquette for Students

Since we make use of the written word to a great extent, email etiquette is important to be a successful student. Especially at larger universities, it is difficult to discuss lessons with professors, at times. As a result, responses from the reader may be delayed, and you do not want to be misunderstood. Therefore, the following components of good email etiquette are presented here.

- Fundamentals
- Tone
- Attachments
- Complaints
- Appropriate email topics
- Inappropriate email topics

The Fundamentals:

1. When emailing a professor, at all times include your **full name, class period or department.**
2. Include your class and what the email is specifically regarding in the subject.
3. Before sending this email, carefully think about the content and its appropriateness because after sending it, it is available on the Internet for anyone to read.
4. Keep the email short (one screen length).

5. Answer all emails in the same time span you would a phone call.
6. Check for spelling, punctuation and grammar errors before clicking Send.
7. Always utilize a professional type font, not decorative.

Tone:

1. Always type in a positive tone: (i.e., <u>When</u> I come to class…, versus, <u>If</u> I come to class…).
2. Keep away from using negatives: (i.e., prefixes - un, non, ex and suffixes – less).
3. Avoid emoticons.

Attachments:

1. When attaching files, it is helpful to include in the email the filename, file format, and the program version. (i.e., *Attached: "ResearchProposal.doc" Microsoft Word 2007.*)
2. It is a good idea to send files in portable document format (pdf) to guarantee compatibility.

Complaints:
1. In a few words, state the complaint's history for context to the reader.
2. Clarify attempts you have made earlier to clear up the problem.
3. Explain the importance of your reader resolving the problem.
4. Offer resolution suggestions and/or other means of helping.

<u>Example</u>

Professor:

It has come to our attention in English 301 that a majority of our class did not pass the midterm examination. We have met as a group to discuss the problem and would like to present our viewpoint to you and your T.A.s. There are underlying causes, which do not include our full knowledge of the material studied, that we need to discuss with you. We thank you for taking our proposal into consideration and look forward to your positive response.

Sincerely,

English 301 Students

Appropriate Email Topics:
1. Questions of your professor that can be briefly answered.
2. Scheduling of appointment with your professor.
3. Homework that you are assigned to submit via email.

Inappropriate Email Topics:
1. When professors have specified to submit assignments in hard copy form, do not email them.
2. When asking for an assignment extension, do it in person.
3. Continuous conversation topics require face-to-face contact.

YOUR NOTES

ANSWER KEY

SECTION 1

Exercise 1-A

1. children

2. will not

3. father

4. and

5. Why?

6. application

7. could not

8. large

9. quotation

10. ride

11. It was quickly eaten.

12. The following data may be considered.

13. He ordered fish, chips, and salad.

14. There are many ways to solve the problem.

Exercise 1-B
Answers will vary; it is your choice. I have given suggested answers.

1. healthy/robust

2. superb/excellent

3. consume eat

4. fully/completely

5. Daily/ Every day

6. prolonged

7. count/gauge

8. during

9. permits

10. belief

Exercise 1-C

1. steaming

2. bake

3. listen

4. watch

5. spooned

6. drew

7. write

8. pulled

9. combed

10. brush

Exercise 1-D

1. vary

2. identify

3. proceed

4. abandon

5. consolidate

6. accumulate

7. illustrate

8. generate

9. derive

10. establish

Exercise 1-E

1. evaluation

2. domain

3. verdict

4. response

5. moderation

6. indignity

7. animation

8. precursor

9. contemplation

10. declaration

Exercise 1-F

1. metropolis

2. nation

3. disease

4. magnitude

5. procedure

6. suggestion

7. article

8. dilemma

9. response

10. lure

Exercise 1-G

1. recollection

2. occurrence

3. revelation

4. blizzard

5. exemplifications

6. compliance

7. distinction

8. divergences

9. prominence

10. proposals

SECTION 2

Exercise 2-A

Answers will vary.

Exercise 2-B

Stephanie Student received the Bachelor of Science Degree in Nursing from the XYZ University, Seoul, South Korea, in 1995, and Master of Science Degree in Adult Nursing from the same university in 2001. From 1995 to 2001, she was at the XX Hospital as a nurse, and she experienced nursing on the medical-surgical ward. From 2001 to 2003, she worked as a researcher and clinical instructor at the College of Nursing, the XYZ University, and she was responsible for undergraduate student clinical instruction of nephrology, pulmonary, and oncology medicine, along with surgery. Also, at that time, she published two articles and delivered oral presentations twice at an international conference. Since the fall of 2004, she has been in the doctoral program of the College of Nursing, XX University. Her department is XX, and her research interest is the health promotion of immigrant elderly women.

Exercise 2-C

Stan Student earned his Bachelor's and Master's of Engineering at the University of XYZ and is currently a full-time Master of Business Administration (MBA) student at the University of ABC. Before starting the MBA study, he worked at various businesses.

This poorly written sample of a biostatement was packed with so many different jobs and educational exploits that it was very difficult to follow and at the same time to believe! My advice for such writing would be to begin all over and highlight only the very important topics. Plus, do not forget about maintaining a logical order to the biostatement, either in chronological or reverse chronological order.

Exercise 2-D

Currently, Steven Student is a graduate student of chemistry at the University of XYZ. He has been involved in several research projects in pharmacology. His research mainly focused on extracting, characterizing, and modifying compounds of pharmaceutical ingredients and antibacterial polymers. He holds a Master's of Science in Biochemistry and Molecular

Science from AB University, PQ, the United States of America, and a Bachelor's of Science in Chemistry from BC. He has worked in DE Pharmaceutical Company and FG Company. He has published two papers and applied for a patent in JK.

SECTION 3

Exercise 3-A

Sample 2

Notably, McCormick Tribune Plaza & Ice Rink is a popular site for many Chicagoans and tourists alike. Specifically, it is situated within Millennium Park just east of Chicago's Loop (business center). As a matter of fact, December 2001 was the inauguration of this first attraction in Millennium Park; graciously, named for the donated funds by the McCormick Tribune Foundation. On a daily basis, the ice rink is free to the general public and remains open in the winter from November to March. During the warmer months, the area is transformed into Chicago's largest open air dining venue, "Park Grill Plaza" offering beautiful views of Millennium Parks' points of interest and gardens.

Exercise 3-B

1. Admittedly,

2. Assuredly, Additionally, Moreover, Also,

3. on the other hand, in contrast, (These are the best choices since you do not want to be redundant by using admittedly and/or assuredly.)

4. Therefore,

5. additionally.

6. clearly then

7. likewise,

8. point in fact, soon,

9. Certainly,

10. Unquestionably, In final consideration, Moreover,

Exercise 3-C

(Answers may vary)

With respect to an ideal geographic location, Nassau, Bahamas, enjoys a very warm climate. Islands in the Caribbean Ocean possess beautiful amenities for tourists. As a matter of fact, St. John and St. Croix maintain beautiful harbors to launch an excursion upon a seafaring yacht. Notably, scuba diving and snorkeling are world renowned here among the clear waters and coral reefs.

Exercise 3-D

(Answers may vary)

While, the Caribbean islands exude warmth and fun in the sun; on the other hand, tourists travel to Saint Petersburg, Russia, for much different reasons. In contrast, this city is known for its marvelous architecture. Instead of sun tanning on the beaches, the sightseers spend their days on walking tours in the city. Rather than packing swim suits and sun tan oil, arrive prepared with good walking shoes and warm clothing. In either case, enjoy your travels either on land or sea.

Exercise 3-E

(Answers may vary)

Tourists must take good care of their health because one would not want to arrive at the destination in poor health. If one sleeps on the plane, drinks plenty of water and exercises the legs, consequently, "jet lag" may be avoided. Therefore, if one feels a bit of "jet lag" after arriving, try to maintain a sensible sleep schedule in the new time zone to acclimate yourself. Thus, in a couple of days one can adapt to the new schedule like a local.

Exercise 3-F

(Answers may vary)

First of all, begin with a suitable itinerary for your trip. Next, search the Internet for fares and lodging, subsequently, comparing the cost, convenience, and schedule of the travel routes. In sum, purchase everything, incidentally, do not forget to update your passport and required visas. Bon voyage!

Exercise 3-G

(Answers may vary)

Chicago winters can be brutally cold and windy; also, our temperatures may drop below zero (Fahrenheit). The Great Lakes greatly affect our wintry weather; furthermore, the strong winds cause a wind chill effect. This wind chill factor is colder than the outside temperature; clearly, leading to how we feel this cold air on our exposed skin due to the wind. One morning, it may be 35 degrees; yet, by afternoon the temperatures may drop by 20 degrees. Always dress for the cold in layers; consequently, that way you will be prepared for changes in weather. Notably, Chicago's winter daytime skies may be crystal clear with a bright sun shining; on the contrary, the temperatures are without doubt freezing cold!

Exercise 3-H

Aaron made his bed; he proceeded to get dressed.

Your e-mail account is not working; I do not know what the problem could be.

It is located on the third floor of the library; the class is scheduled for 4 PM on Tuesdays.

Our bus was late; we decided to walk to school.

Let's go swimming at the beach; it's such a beautiful sunny day.

Traffic is backed up from the rain; everyone was late to work.

Exercise 3-I

1. transformation
2. situations
3. times
4. enthusiasm

SECTION 4

Exercise 4-A

Paul wanted to take an automobile trip through the United States Appalachian Mountains, so he and his brother began making plans on his Dell computer. They routed their journey from Chicago, Illinois, east through Indiana and began their mountain climbing in Kentucky. Tennessee was the next state to hike; meandering their way toward North Carolina's beautiful mountaintop ranges. Once they reached the state of Virginia, Paul was complaining of sore feet. Yet, the two brothers were able to complete their journey by enjoying the mountain peaks of the Maryland Appalachians.

Exercise 4-B

The ever popular American jeans were crafted by two immigrants in the latter part of the 19th century. Originally, Jacob Davis and Levi Strauss designed this rugged wear for _0_ farm hands who worked the land from sun-up to sun-down. Denim fabric proved to withstand the brutal work these pants were subjected to on a regular basis. "Waist overalls" were the original name for these pants, and it was not until the 1960s when the "baby boomer generation" made them popular and began calling them blue jeans. Today around the world, one can find jeans in style just about anywhere.

Exercise 4-C

Skateboarding has developed over the last sixty-odd years into a very popular sport throughout the U.S.A. It all began in California when surfers decided to bring their sport to the streets. Initially, they attempted simple construction with a smaller wooden surfboard along with front and back roller skates. As the surfers navigated the street's pavement while having fun, they continued to improve upon the design of their original model. During the early years of skateboarding, experimentation ruled the sport from its infancy. Eventually, _0__boards and wheels were highly refined into the ever popular skateboards we see today.

Exercise 4-D

(Answers may vary)

a bridge	a computer virus	a laser
a conductor a mentor/advisor	a carcinogen (cancer causing agent)	
a piano	a landfill (buried trash)	a residence hall or dormitory

A mentor/advisor is a learned person who uses his/her wisdom to guide others.

Exercise 4-E

1. A catalyst is a substance that can speed up the rate of a chemical reaction without changing its own structure.

2. A black hole is a celestial body with approximately the same mass as the sun and a gravitational radius of about 3 km.

3. Heat is a form of energy which can be transmitted through solid and liquid media by conduction.

4. A brake is a device capable of slowing the motion of a mechanism.

5. A dome is generally a hemispherical roof on top of a circular, square, or other-shaped structure.

6. A piccolo is a small flute pitched an octave higher than a standard flute.

Exercise 4-F

(Answers may vary)

1. A thermometer is an instrument by which temperature can be measured.

2. Photosynthesis is a process by which sunlight is used to manufacture carbohydrates from water and carbon dioxide.

3. A credit bureau is an organization in which businesses can apply for financial information on potential customers.

4. An anhydride is a compound of which the elements of water have been removed.

5. An eclipse is a celestial event in which one body, such as a star, is covered by another, such as a planet.

6. An axis is an imaginary line on which a body is said to rotate.

Exercise 4-G

Please reduce the following if possible grammatically or stylistically.

1. Section 6 is devoted to numerical examples demonstrating the necessity of the line source models.

2. Chinatown is a tourist attraction that serving as an introduction to Chinese culture and cuisine for other residents of the city.

3. One of the principal challenges facing public health professionals is to determine the factors influencing, facilitating, and then maintaining exercise participation in a majority of the older population.

4. Sixteen Chinese restaurant owners/managers will be randomly selected from a list which will be provided by the Chinatown Chamber of Commerce.

5. The proportion of older individuals regularly participating in physical activity is disappointingly low.

6.   Two studies noted areas with a high prevalence of HIV; male circumcision was not traditionally practiced.

SECTION 5

Exercise 5-A

1. What type of information is included in each of the sentences?

sentence #1 Navigation is a process by which means of transport can be guided to their destination when the route has few or no landmarks.
    definition

sentence #2 Some of the earliest navigators were sailors, who steered their ships first by the stars, then with a compass, and later with more complicated instruments that measured the position of the sun.
    support

sentence #3 We are reminded of this by the fact that the word navigation comes from the Latin word for "ship."
    support

sentence #4 However, the history and importance of navigation changed radically in the twentieth century with the development of aircraft and missiles which fly in three dimensions.
    support

sentence #5 Today, both ships and aircraft rely heavily on computerized navigational systems that can provide a continuous, immediate, and accurate report of position.
    conclusion

2. How is the passage organized?

It is organized from general to specific, ending with a more general current statement.

3. What verb tenses are used for which sentences? Why?

Navigation is a process by which means of transport can be guided to their destination when the route has few or no landmarks.
The first sentence is present tense since it defines navigation for now and forever.

Some of the earliest navigators were sailors, who steered their ships first by the stars, then with a compass, and later with more complicated instruments that measured the position of the sun.
The second sentence is historical; therefore, the past tense is used.

We are reminded of this by the fact that the word navigation comes from the Latin word for "ship."
The third sentence remains in the past tense since it explains how the word originally developed.

However, the history and importance of navigation changed radically in the twentieth century with the development of aircraft and missiles which fly in three dimensions.
The fourth sentence continues in the past tense since it is ongoing with historical information.

Today, both ships and aircraft rely heavily on computerized navigational systems that can provide a continuous, immediate, and accurate report of position.
The fifth and last sentence returns to the present tense since it is descriptive in relating to today's navigation.

4. Sentence three begins with we. Is this appropriate?

No, stay in the third person.

Mindful of this fact, the word navigation comes from the Latin word for "ship."

Exercise 5-B

<u>General Sentences</u>   1 & 5   <u>Specific Sentences</u> 2, 3, & 4

Exercise 5-C

___3___   In the not too distant past, we marveled at how TV phenomenally connected us with others so far away, but people are enjoying this new technology in novel forms of contact.

___1___   The Internet has expanded our horizons in astounding ways that affect the world's population.

___7___   Our future will reveal Internet wonders beyond our imagination.

___2___   This effect is bringing people closer than ever before through travel and the World Wide Web.

___4___   Communication has been streamlined with data packages that allow one to connect by cell phone, texting, and social media which may lead to a whole other topic of romance.

___6___   For instance, no longer will you need to go shopping for an engagement ring at the jewelry store downtown, when online shopping is so much more convenient.

___5___   Dating online has redefined the whole meaning of meeting someone with common interests, developing a meaningful relationship, and perhaps making a commitment.

Exercise 5-D

Palindromes

___2___The term itself comes from the ancient Greek word palindromos meaning "running back again".

___4___Another good and more recent example is "If I had a Hi-Fi."

___3___Some very common English words are palindromes, such as pop, dad, and noon.

___1___A palindrome is a word or phrase that results in the same sequence of letters whether it is read from left to right or from right to left.

___5___One of the classic long palindromes is "A man, a plan, a canal, Panama."

___6___Long palindromes are very hard to construct, and some word puzzlers spend immense amounts of time trying to produce good examples.

Exercise 5-E

1. computer   analysis of components/elements & exemplification

2. university   analysis of components/elements & exemplification

3. screen saver   knowledge of applications, exemplification

4. Viking   exemplification & historical change & development

5. software   analysis of components/elements, knowledge of applications, exemplification

6. advertising   analysis of components/elements, knowledge of applications, exemplification

Exercise 5-F
(Answers will vary)

America's International Students

(Specific) Support #1:

American universities are well noted for excellent programs in higher education and welcome these highly motivated students.

(Specific) Support #2:

At first, the American style of educating may seem quite different from their homeland's instruction, but after one semester, they are easily assimilated into the mainstream of the university.

(Specific) Support #3:

These students truly add a diverse dimension to our campuses and become vital resources in their fields of study.

Exercise 5-G
(Answers will vary)

Topic Sentence: The United States of America has a beautifully diverse land mass made up of four distinct areas.

Concluding Sentence: As you can see, America offers a variety of weather and diverse land forms.

SECTION 6

Exercise 6-A

a. 5
b. 2
c. 4
d. 1
e. 6
f. 3
g. 7

Exercise 6-B

1. Physical chemistry is probably important for marital bliss.

2. Defensive driving tends to be ineffective.

3. Over-eating most likely causes human beings to become over weight.

4. Rain storms may cause flooding.

5. Rest and drinking fluids may be the best remedy to recover from the flu.

6. Swimming is likely the best exercise for working all parts of the human body.

7. Great novels tend to be written by Russian authors.

8. Preschools assist children in usually becoming better overall students.

Exercise 6-C

Answers will vary.

Exercise 6-D

1. proportion
2. Japanese males tend to develop digestive cancer.
3. This may tend to have a relationship with their appetite tendency.
4. suggest, tend, may tend

Exercise 6-E

Answers will vary.

SECTION 7

Exercise 7-A

    1. U
    2. A
    3. U
    4. A
    5. A
    6. U

Exercise 7-B

    1. paraphrase A
    2. paraphrase B
    3. paraphrase B

Exercise 7-C

Answers will vary.

Exercise 7-D

    1. a
    2. a
    3. b
    4. c and d
    5. c

Exercise 7-E

    1. are superior
    2. have faulty connections
    3. feels better
    4. can cure stress
    5. can insure jobs

Exercise 7-F

1. P-1, Americans work too much.
   P-2, extra overtime
   P-3, recession, lay-offs
   P-4, trading income for time

2. paragraph number one

3. "Since World War II, Americans are working more hours than ever before."

SECTION 8

Exercise 8-A

Answers will vary.

Exercise 8-B

Answers will vary.

Exercise 8-C

Answers will vary.

Exercise 8-D

1. 3
2. 2
3. 4
4. 1

Exercise 8-E

1. The abstract's introduction is fine as it succinctly presents the paper's objectives, except from then on, it goes downward.

2. The author writes in the first person (e.g. "We explain...," "We discuss...," "We comment...," etc.).

3. Results are not specified, and the paper's organization is expressed in very simple terminology.

Example: "Subsequently, we describe... We comment specifically on what students thought were the most important aspects of their experience in architectural capstone design..."

Instead, the abstract should summarize the actual results and how they were obtained.

Example:

"A statistical analysis was performed on answers to survey questions posed to students enrolled in a capstone design course at a major American university. The analysis showed that students thought the most important aspects of their experience in architectural capstone design were quality of the instructor and quantity of student/instructor interaction time."

Exercise 8-F

Answers may vary.

1. objective/s
2. methods
3. results
4. meaning
5. How this research will benefit the domain.
6. Key words introduced.

Exercise 8-G

Sentence 1   introduction
Sentence 2   methods
Sentence 3   objective
Sentence 4   methods
Sentence 5   results
Sentence 6   results
Sentence 7   conclusion

SECTION 9

Exercise 9-A

Answers will vary per topic.

Exercise 9-B

Answers will vary per topic.

Exercise 9-C

Answers will vary per topic.

Exercise 9-D

Answers will vary per topic.

Exercise 9-E

Answers will vary per topic.

SECTION 10

Exercise 10-A

Answers will vary.

Exercise 10-B

Answers will vary.

SECTION 11

Exercise 11-A

Answers will vary.

Exercise 11-B

1. F
2. F
3. F
4. T
5. F
6. T
7. F
8. T
9. T
10. F
11. T
12. T

SECTION 12

Exercise 12-A

Answers will vary.

Exercise 12-B

Answers will vary.

Exercise 12-C

Answers will vary.

YOUR NOTES

ABOUT THE AUTHOR

Audrey Zenner has taught English as a second language for over thirty years to thousands of students from a multitude of lands. As a second language learner herself, (Spanish & German) she easily relates to the language learning progression of her students. For the past five years, she has instructed international graduate students at the University of Illinois at Chicago (UIC). Through her students' suggestions during the UIC Academic Writing for International Graduate Students class, which meets both fall and spring semesters, Audrey presents this text in hopes that it will assist in your own academic writing.

She holds a Bachelor's Degree in Education/Language Arts/Spanish and a Master's Degree in Linguistics/TESOL. With scholarship awards for consecutive years from the State of Illinois, Audrey graduated from the Illinois system of state universities and feels privileged to give back through teaching for the largest state-funded public research university in Chicago with approximately 28,000 students. Before UIC, she taught ESL through the community colleges surrounding Chicago. She is an active member of the Illinois Teachers of English to Speakers of Other Languages-Bilingual Education (ITBE), an affiliate of TESOL, an international organization. Plus, articles on course materials have been published by Audrey in the ITBE Link.